Iron Sharpens Iron

"Inspired To Achieve, Think, & Grow,"

Volume II

DR. LARRY WHITE SR.
JACKIE "HOLLYWOOD" MIMS
LISA JONES HARWELL
R. WESLEY WEBB

COPYRIGHTS

Copyright © 2021 by Dr. Larry White Sr. All right reserved.

In accordance with the U.S. Copyright Acts of 1976, no part of this publication may be reproduced, distributed or transmitted in any form or by other electronic or mechanical method without prior expressed permission of the author, except in the case of brief quotations embodied in critical reviews and other commercial uses permitted by copyright laws. Thank you for your support of the author's rights.

Author by Dr. Larry White Sr.

Redbaby Publishing, Inc., Clinton, MD 20735

eBook ISBN 9781952163098

Paperback ISBN 9781952163104

TABLE OF CONTENTS

- You'd Betta Recognize!...13
  Leah Chapman
- Deposit Your Dreams Into Success.................................18
  Dr. Larry White Sr.
- Don't "Weight" for your Wake-Up Call…………………..22
  Tiffany Williams-Parra
- Fisher of Men ………………………………………….......27
  Eric A. Lomax
- Breaking Through Traditional Thinking…………………..33
  Demetrica "Meechie" Jefferis

- **Wise Counsel** 37

  R. R. Wesley Webb

- **Smart Women Finish Strong** 46

  Gina Goree-Hitchens

- **Reinvented by His Design** 53

  Lisa Jones Harwell

- **Perseverance: The Key to Resilience & Leading Through Challenging Times** 57

  Eve Gomez

- **The Neuro Black-Out** 61

  Dr. Paul W. Dyer

- Beyond Loss……………………………………………………………66
  Cortne' Lee Smith

- Taking Your Great To Greater: Level UP……………………69
  Dr. Clarice Kavanaugh

- Build Generational Wealth Starts in the Mind………………73
  Toya Jordan

- Finding MY IT!…77
  Senita V. Carter

- Black History Sharpens American History………………..……81
  Vincent O. Leggett

- Place Respect on My Name……………………………………..… 85
  Charlemagne McCarter

- Living in the Moment……………………………………………89
  Natalie Degraffinreaidt

- Faith, Hope & Love Part II, Exercise Your Faith Daily… 93
  Jackie "Hollywood" Mims

INTRODUCTION

Bestselling Author Lisa Jones Harwell

"The Infinity Circle,"

If I had to find the one perfect adjective to describe the authors of this anthology, illustrious members of Signature Entrepreneurs and Masterminds Group, I would fall short. How would one mesh brilliant, fierce, excellence, diligent, resilient and God-fearing into one word? Each individual, featured between the covers of this book, is an elite paragon. Although each of us has traveled a different path on our journey called life, we share one common goal "to be of service."

"As iron sharpens iron, so one person sharpens another" comes from Proverbs, 27:17. This is not just about critiquing and providing guidance from one man to another, or to a group of individuals. There is a process, a method in which we learn, we communicate, socialize, and work. Some of these members discovered their purpose and passion early, while others took a few winding roads. The result is the same. We all answered God's calling not only to be of service, but to mentor like-minded individuals along the way. Using our instruction of courtesy, be clear and concise in our communication, we sharpen each other through mentoring and prayer to be a better servant, entrepreneur, community leader and human being. Like the African proverbs "Each one, teach one" and "It takes a village," I am proud of this village, in which I am a member of.

We often hear the phrase "no man is an island unto himself." We did not learn to talk alone, walk alone or learn alone. Signature Entrepreneurs and Masterminds is an infinity circle. As a noun, infinity refers to a state of unlimited extent, boundless (Merriam-Webster). Our support of each other is infinite. If one sees a kink in the armor, we rally and provide the strength, the reinforcement to make it strong again. Every member is my friend, my brother, my sister, my colleague, my prayer warrior and mentor.

May the words that follow bless you abundantly. May it provide you with insight, laughter, grace and courage. Use and refer to it often to restore your armor, to give you hope when you need peace or encouragement to continue on or try again. Humbly, I present to you *Volume II "Iron Sharpens Iron" Inspired to Achieve, Think and Grow*.

PREFACE
Bestselling Author R. Wesley Webb

The idea of creating a piece of literature that amalgamated motivation, inspiration and passion into one for its readers appealed to me when I realized how greatly other similar works of literature helped me grow and evolve. Literary works such as *Into the Heart of Mindfulness* by Ed Halliwell, *The Art of Happiness* by Dalai Lama, and *Laws of Success* by Napoleon Hill assisted me when I felt like giving up. Therefore, when the opportunity arose to contribute to this anthology along with the other members of the Signature Entrepreneur and Mastermind group, I felt a real since of purpose in helping any individual who might be stuck in finding their way professionally or finding what motivates them to be their best in life. I hope that Iron Sharpens Iron brings a smile to your face and courage to your heart.

Even the greatest minds in history had struggled with the inability to go on in their life when they came face to face with circumstances that tore their relief away from them. I believe one does not grow without problems because experiencing the effects of a challenge you cannot overcome easily is what provides you with the motivation, wisdom, and strength to find the right solution.

Similarly, Ed Halliwell struggled with anxiety and depression during his twenties and early thirties. His constant effort to understand and overcome the distress he felt every single day.

However, when he stumbled upon meditation and Buddhism, he discovered a different path from the other medical, psychological, and spiritual cures he had tried previously. That path that he had found took him into the heart of mindfulness, and its practice transformed his life, easing his depression and helping him see each moment as precious.

Ed's life changed completely, and then he shared his secret to benefit everyone by teaching mindfulness to others. In his book, Ed explores how mindfulness can enable us to see and transform our unhelpful prejudices and habits, empower us to live more at peace with stress and uncertainty, foster hopefulness and understanding. He found it could help us find our life's calling—if we are prepared to journey to the heart of the practice.

The number of people like Ed Halliwell, who did not hold back in sharing their secret to success with the rest of the world, can be counted on one's fingers. Napoleon Hill is surely among them.

I believe that Napoleon Hill is one of the greatest founders of the motivational and self-development rhetoric. His work is a treasure trove of ideas that continue to inspire decades after they were first published. In his classics, Napoleon talks about a person's inner aura. By putting it into words, he maintains a good vantage point to evaluate the effectiveness of one's actions. The teachings that he has gifted to the world have enabled many people to change their perspective about how the world works and who they are as individuals.

The 14th Dalai Lama, whose work is indeed a source of inspiration for millions of people all over the world, is someone who shared his secret to achieving fulfillment by motivating several others to do the same. In his book, "The Art of Happiness", Dalai Lama shared that happiness is attained by preserving peace with others and one's self, which can be relinquished through meditation and community service. Therefore, he concluded that our purpose isn't to create stress but a positive atmosphere. This gives our life meaning, which leads to complete contentment.

I, too, have learned a thing or two about life, and the role models who I look up to inspire me to share what I've learned with all of you; as anyone can become successful, but only a few people can assist many others in becoming successful as well. True happiness lies at the heart of contentment, and for me, contentment comes once you achieve what you put your mind to, and then share that knowledge with several others who have the same goals as you.

In fact, even if one has different goals than you, my belief is that happiness is everyone's aim. Whether they believe their job brings them joy or money enables them to feel uplifted. The goal is to achieve happiness.

Iron sharpens iron is a proverb that means that one man helps sharpen another. The main idea behind the anthology is the fact that the entire human population will find more ease in reaching their individualistic goals if everyone was to help each other get there. Most often, help can be provided by a single word, a pat on the back, or encouragement. I found my way forward because I had the privilege of receiving ample advice throughout my childhood and early adult life from many wonderful individuals.

I would like to compile that very advice and present it to you as a little gift for believing that tomorrow is always better and pondering stories in this book. Trust me when I say a little advice goes a long way.

I contributed to this book because there are thousands of people who are still finding their true purpose and understanding how they can work towards achieving it. Having benefitted from the advice and helping hands, I consider it to be my purpose to share what I've learned so far with all of them. I have seen life up close, and I want my story to be a source of motivation for anyone who currently feels like they are constantly failing, failing to get up in the morning for work, failing to smile even when they feel like it and failing to become the best possible version of themselves.

You create your success, but in order to do that, you must first figure out what the definition of success is for you. What is success for you? What does it mean? Once you know where you want to be, it will be ten folds easier to get there. Identifying your purpose in life is crucial because everyone has a different purpose. Different things bring different people happiness. Searching for success without knowing what it specifically means to you is like finding a needle in a haystack with the lights out.

When you finally identify what success means to you, you will set goals. This will provide you with a sense of direction, clarity, and targets. Believe me, when you walk in the direction that will lead you to fulfilling your dreams, you will come across many obstacles. But you will have to learn how to use those very obstacles as stepping stones in order to climb the ladder to contentment; every step matters.

Success isn't the name of a destination. Success is the journey that you embark on when you decide you want to accomplish a goal that is unique. Every step along the way embeds a bit of success. Every fall, every failure is always a step ahead, and that's what we often forget. Failure itself is a step forward, as it teaches you which path not to take.

Through this book, I would like to convey that it is never too late to pick up where you left off and start moving ahead. It is never too late to take another path. Don't be afraid of change; don't be afraid of time running out. Time is put to waste when you are stuck at the same point for a long period. You won't be wasting time if you spend it trying to achieve what you've always wanted.

As Napoleon Hill said, you can become what you perceive yourself to be. Perceive yourself in a light that helps you believe in yourself while pushing you to improve at the same time. I want this book to become a guide for people to understand and improve themselves, each other, and the life they lead.

You will face several problems when you try to improve yourself and the environment you function in. Understanding the problem is key to solving the problem. Hence, I would like to invite you to a glorious, enlightening, and transformative journey with me and the other contributors through certain events in our lives that became unforgettable lessons which we seek to convey to you through this anthology.

FOREWARD
Bestselling Author Jackie "Hollywood" Mims

Dr. Larry White Sr birthed a uniquely designed extraordinary organization: Signature Entrepreneur and Mastermind. His dream and passion are to cultivate individuals with gifts and talents to share with each other ideas, thoughts and develop a practical application to their personal development and insight into their growth.

Iron Sharpens Iron II
The Proverbs Vision

A Proverb is a parable, maxim, or allegory. It is a verb that means to compare or to be similar. Proverbs also suggest truth comparing similar experiences and circumstances. Some suggest that Proverbs is a short saying containing a nugget of truth. *Iron Sharpens Iron II* are stories of individuals sharing their own personal truths designed to uplift the reader. These are individuals who have overcome trials, struggles, pain, and suffering to achieve a complication of life stories designed to encourage and motivate the person reading the book.

Iron Sharpen Irons II, The Proverbs Vision *"As Iron Sharpen Iron, So a man sharpens the countenance of his friend"* There are critical components in the sharpening process. Iron is an extremely tough substance so are some experiences the authors had to overcome to create this book. The context, moments of reflection, and personal pain directly affected the creation of this book. From a personal experience, my mom was fighting for her life when I wrote Faith, Hope, and Love the final chapter of Iron Sharpens Iron Volume I. My iron was watching the impact of COVID-19 had on the love of my life with every breath for her life. I had to gather my strength in the Lord to write the chapter dedicated to the life and legacy of Frances "Nana" Mims. That was my Iron which was sharpened by Dr. Larry White who spoke words of encouragement into my life and motivated me to write at the darkest hour in my life.

When a person sharpens the countenance of another, they elevate, equip, and motivate each other through difficult and challenging times.

It's often said that greatness is individuals who do not follow a path but make a trail for others to follow. I believe ***Iron Sharpens Iron II*** makes a trail for individuals to follow through with their daily struggles. These extraordinary writers will affect the minds of readers and trigger them to take introspection and encourage the reader to build and continue to dream big.

You will be amazed and empowered after reading their stories. What is your Iron and how do you find the tools to sharpen your Iron so that you can become the absolute best you? Conversely, who can you lift positively so that your Iron can sharpen someone else? We have Irons in the fire that needs to be sharpened. There is greatness in the pages of this book. This is truly a plethora of characteristics that describe entrepreneurs. Read it and become inspired, apply the inspiration to your life, and be changed.

"But they that wait upon the Lord…shall renew their strength; they shall mount up with wings as eagles; they shall run, and not be weary; and they shall walk, and not faint."

Isaiah 40:31

Jackie "Hollywood" Mims

www.jackiemims.com

Our Motta

***

Creating Vision

&

Creating Partnerships

ACKNOWLEDGEMENTS

Dion Banks

Bestselling Author | Community Leader

On behalf of the entire Mastermind Group, we would like to take this time to express our extreme gratitude for your gracious monetary donations to this compilation and your countless hours planning with Signature Entrepreneurs & Masterminds. Dion has been an intricate part of our recent success leading us in Economic Development and Empowerment. Your talents and skill set are unparalleled throughout the country. Again, we thank you for your hard work and dedication and always "Operating in Excellence".

ACKNOWLEDGEMENTS

Sherry DeVouse-Dennard

Bestselling Author | Insurance Broker

Signature Entrepreneurs & Masterminds
recognize Sherry as a constant professional

within our organization. Your recent contributions have been an extreme blessing to our programs and events. It honored us to award you with our prestigious Mastermind leadership award for 2021. We have extremely appreciated your strive for excellence in your future endeavors and remember that your leadership to our organization. You are truly the Iron that sharpens Iron with a process of bottom-line results.

Leah D. Mills-Chapman, LMSW

Clinical Therapist | Author | Entrepreneur

You'd Betta Recognize!

Leah D. Mills-Chapman, LMSW (aka "The Mental Reconstructionist") is a Licensed Clinical Therapist. She is a two-time graduate of the University of Michigan–Ann Arbor, where she received a Bachelor of Arts Degree in Psychology and African American Studies, as well as, a Master of Social Work Degree, with a concentration in Mental Health and Interpersonal Practice. Leah began her practice working with the

You'd Betta Recognize!

most vulnerable populations in America–persons addicted to substances, women with HIV, and juveniles incarcerated in high secure facilities, all of which were predominantly African American (Black) clients. This work led her to study more about what was driving such harmful, high-risk behaviors and identified trauma as being a major factor. Leah received state certification and specializes in traumatology. This rigorous training assists Leah in transforming the lives of severely, emotionally disturbed individuals and family systems. In addition, she has used this tutelage and assisted social systems and companies in transforming their environment into ones that are emotionally safe and culturally inclusive spaces. Leah D. Mills, LMSW is the Chief Executive Officer of Ntervene, LLC. She is a sought-after consultant, trainer, speaker, lecturer and clinical supervisor of other professionals in mental health and wellness, including trauma-informed/focused practices. She has a proven rate of transformative success.

On a more personal note, Leah is the wife of one husband and the mother of four beautiful young adults. She is no stranger to the dysfunction found in ALL family systems and the stress and trauma that comes along with being a part of them. This awareness drives her work of service to others, hoping they will find healing and discover their inner peace. While helping others, Leah finds a few moments to take care of her mind, body, and spirit. She loves to sing, shop, watch comedy, relax with her family and pampered, occasionally. Leah is a lover and disciple of God. She believes that something divinely shaped her life for rendering hope to the hopeless by being a living testimony. So, Leah lives each intentional day doing her part.

You'd Betta Recognize!

I remember it rather vividly… The time that I had wandered away from my mother's side while shopping at Kmart. There were some eye-catching toys I wanted to explore, while my mother was perusing about looking at the boring stuff… like laundry detergent and toilet tissue. I was 6 years old! What 6-year-old child wants to go shopping for household products? Not me! So, I walked out into the sea of people, unaware of any impending danger, in search of my coveted toys. The allure of the colorful toy section was so strong and had such a magnetic pull I did not recognize just how far I was from the one that had my best interest at heart and made certain that they protected me from harm. I became frantic and cried aloud, "MOMMY…MOMMY"! But I was so far out of earshot that she could not detect my tiny voice and cries. This left me panicked! I continued to wander, not knowing where I was going.

    Moments later, a strange woman came up to me and said, "Little girl… are you lost"? I replied, "Yes, Ma'am. I'm looking for my Mommy". This kind woman assured me that all would be well and asked the name of my mother and then me. I didn't have on a name badge, like she did. I could identify who it based her on this visual signifier, but she had no clue who I was from sight. So, I answered her and said with great confidence, "My mommy's name is Patricia Mills and my name is Leah Mills". The lady repeated back to me what I had said and then asked for me to follow her. As nervous as I was, because of the well-known phrase–me "Stranger Danger"–my only option was to trust her in this emergent time of need. I walked with her to the front desk and she spoke into a microphone. She said, "Patricia Mills to the front desk… Patricia Mills to the front desk". And

You'd Betta Recognize!

within seconds, my mother appeared! Oh, the relief that I felt inside. Once I heard her voice and then saw her face. I knew I was going to be alright.

Now what would have happened if my mother had never taken out the time to teach me, in my earlier years, my complete name? In that moment of tragedy, when asked by the store assistant to identify myself, I would not have been able to tell her my name. And what if my mother did not recognize her name being called over the loudspeaker? I may have never been reunited with my mother and thus the other members of my family. Both scenarios would have ended in sheer devastation for me. In the Biblical text which grounds the basis of this anthology — "Iron Sharpens Iron"—it states, "As iron sharpens iron, so one person sharpens another"- Proverbs 27:17 (NIV). In the aforementioned story, my mother taught me, in my formative years, who I was. She reinforced in my mind that my name was Leah Mills. My mother was an iron, and she invested in sharpening me, so that in moments where I needed to be seen, I knew who I was — "A Mills." But if asked if I was an iron, would I have been aware?

In my study of the shared text, it led me to the salient realization of there being a process that happens for a person to become sharp. But then I looked deeper into the text and through prayer and meditation, the Holy Spirit revealed to me that before you can partake in becoming greater than you are, right now, you must know, with all certainty, WHO YOU ARE. You know you are an iron! So, before you can begin the refinement or

You'd Betta Recognize!

sharpening process, you must have self-awareness and self-recognition. Many lack these important traits.

As a Licensed Clinical Therapist in Mental Health, I often work with people that face identity confusion, questioning, and even loss. For so long, they have operated in roles designed for them. They had no input into the description of the role and no choice in whether they wanted to fulfill the role. They were simply put there by another's selfish desires and made to perform. This type of hegemonic rule happens within dysfunctional family systems. Yes... I know... You weren't shaped within a dysfunctional family system. OF COURSE NOT! Maladaptive thought #1! We ALL have emerged out of some level of familial dysfunction. Now YOUR dysfunction may not look like MY dysfunction, but it is STILL DYSFUNCTION, nonetheless. So, if one would allow themselves to be honest, they will see that most of their identity has been shaped by the external input of another person. Sadly, they will acknowledge that their thoughts, feelings and decisions were omitted from the outcome of who they are today.

When one becomes powerless and loses any semblance of autonomy, they will succumb to the complete will and dominance of others. This unfortunate reality allows other individuals to have power and control over how another may view themselves. What they feel about themselves? How they think of themselves? What messages and self-talk they may speak to themselves; and thus, the value placed on themselves. In time, they will find that they are functioning at a deficit in true self-awareness. Many times, in therapy, I say to my clients,

You'd Betta Recognize!

"What are your strengths? Please name 3-5 of them". Often, they struggle immensely to identify just one. I validate their difficulty to see the power within and then quickly shift to the next question. "Can you name 3-5 of your weaknesses"? It is at this point that I see how efficient they are in either seeing every flaw that they may have, or they are still in a space of identifying no value of self and are operating from a space of no self-worth. This is a critical moment that shows just how badly they are unaware of the strength and beauty within. They have no recollection of who they truly are… a masterpiece of the Almighty Creator.

Now, although I can identify "iron-like" traits–strong, intelligent, beautiful, courageous, and more–within each one of my clients, if I called them an "Iron" without their prior recognition of their "iron-like" traits, my words would all be for naught; They would have no value. "Hey! You are amazing!", I exclaimed…only to hear the soft-spoken voice of my client, "No, I'm not…You can't be talking to me. I ain't nothing. At least, that's what my Mama kept telling me. She would tell me, almost EVERY SINGLE DAY, that I wasn't nothing… just like my no, good Daddy". This example sheds light on the ever so frequent exchanges that are often shared in initial therapy sessions. New clients often repel my words of affirmation, simply because they have never been told from those that should have loved and cared for them early in their lives, that they were an "Iron". It will not be until the individual has a trusted person, who will help them look introspectively through a lens of honesty, will they know they are full of "iron" properties. This such trusted person is me– Leah D. Mills-Chapman, LMSW.

You'd Betta Recognize!

At the start of therapy, most clients are unaware that they have met an "Iron", because they've never been around one and they don't consider themselves one. They have no model of what an "Iron" looks like. You know the old saying, "It takes one to know one"? Well, in this instance, I know that many will only recognize that I am an "Iron" after I assist them through their stages of change. Once they recognize a shift in their negative working model of self, to one that is more positive...the influence of my presence, as a Clinician and their trusted person, will allow for them to better understand that they have been in the company of an "Iron". This revelation will bring awareness that they are being refashioned, refined, emboldened and sharpened into the "Iron" that God purposed them to be.

As a Licensed Clinical Therapist and The CEO of Ntervene, LLC, I assist individuals in rebuilding what's broken...starting with the head. This is an ongoing discovery and developmental process of one's internal strength, by confronting negative core beliefs and past traumatic reminders that continue to speak a painfully false narrative into their reality. Absent this clinical process, sadly, many will continue to wander through life with a lasting, deprecating negative belief of themselves. They will lose out on the opportunity to truly self-actualize and live life to the fullest. The same goes with corporations, organizations and social systems. The longer they continue to exist without acknowledging and confronting internal issues that emerge from unmanaged stressors within their workforce, they will quickly see that they no longer are operating as an "Iron" and need refining and sharpening.

You'd Betta Recognize!

If you desire to function at your optimum level and need help with drawing out and developing your "iron-like traits", with the purpose of knowing exactly who you are, showing up mightily in your own life and the lives of others around you, I admonish you to contact me TODAY… DO NOT HESITATE! Your life and your legacy depend on it.

Leah D. Mills-Chapman, LMSW
"The Mental Reconstructionist"
CEO | Clinical Therapist | Consultant | Trainer | Keynote Speaker
Ntervene, LLC
Website: Ntervene.com
Email info@ntervene.com
Business Phone: 734.480.8065
Social Media Platforms: Facebook, LinkedIn, Instagram, Twitter

Dr. Larry White, Sr.
4X Bestselling Author | Visionary Author

Deposit Your Dreams Into Success

"Dream, Desire, & Determination,"

Deposit Your Dreams Into Success | "Dream, Desire, & Determination"

Dr. White was born in Gary, Indiana and is the youngest of three children and his parents are the late great Sam & Joyce Kikalos. Raised in a middle-class home, Dr. White had his fair share of beginnings in an urban city with a lot of economic challenges as youth growing up in the hometown of Pop Superstar Michael Jackson. Growing up as a kid you always heard of the struggles of the Jackson 5 as their father Joe Jackson was a steel mill worker at the same plant as my dad! By the time of I was 10 years of age, The Jackson had moved to California reaching much success as a family with many awards and accolades while my dad continued to work in the same steel mill factory. I was so proud of my dad on how he carried himself, his work ethic, and his desire to be the best Father He Could Be. The most important thing I learned from my dad was **commitment** and **family**. Always be committed to the ones you love and strive for excellence for the next generation of leaders. My Dad would work in that Steel Mill for 40 years, providing for his family and illustrating strength of family. Today, I set with the following accomplishments leaning on the shoulder of my Father:

- 2021 Gracing the Cover of "You Own It Magazine"
- 2021 International | National Chairman of Signature Entrepreneurs & Mastermind Group
- 2020 Recognition for Dedication & Loyalty from #SEMS
- 2020 4x Bestselling Author & Publisher

- 2019 Keynote Speaker for Maryland's Eastern Shore Black History Program
- 2018 Received Doctorate Degree from WWMI Bible Institute & Seminary
- Mr. White held various mentoring sessions for youth in AACPS to include his Annual Black History Program focusing on Financial Literacy and Entrepreneurship
- 2017 Distributed Back Packs, Toys for over 500 youth & families in various counties throughout the state of Maryland
- 2016 Corporate Leadership Chairman at Microsoft Headquarters in Reston, VA
- 2016 Featured in the Huffington Post for Outstanding Entrepreneurs in Baltimore Region
- 2015 Entrepreneurs Gala Committee Chair BWI Hilton
- 2015 Executive Board Member for Congressional Black Caucus California Delegation
- 2015 Featured Southern Dallas Magazine & Baltimore Times for Entrepreneur of the Year with Emmitt Smith & Steve Harvey
- 2015 Multiple Appearance Radio & Television Stations across the Country.

As I close with my biography, I want to thank all the Contributing Authors. The Signature Entrepreneurs & Masterminds are the pillars for Small Business Owners. Testimonies, creativity, and resources shared in this anthology will forever be engraved in the fiber of African American culture. Each writer has had the daunting task of writing their chapter amid this horrific Pandemic and Racially divided

Deposit Your Dreams Into Success | "Dream, Desire, & Determination"

country, but yet and still they have overcome these obstacles with this new book called "Iron Sharpens Iron, Inspired To Achieve Think & Grow." So, sit back, relax, and enjoy each chapter!

In everyday life, everything starts with a dream, but it is actions behind those dreams to make those dreams come to fruition. Since I was a youth growing up in the urban areas of Northwest Indiana, I dreamed a lot, wondering if I would ever be successful or travel, speak another language, make something of myself. I kept dreaming as I matriculated through middle school and high school. In 1987, I found myself in San Diego, California, looking back at all my dreams from my childhood. The No.1 thing was to make Mom proud!

Dream

In life, everything starts with a dream or some sort of aspiration to be better and achieve greatness in your life and with all dreams, there are expectations. I believe the dream starts with positive mindset to better and make others better around you. Once your dreams are a solid foundation in your heart and mind, you can begin the work to make dreams become reality. It is also important to write your ideas along with dates and deadlines in efforts to stay on track with your greatness. Also, find a mentor who can assist with your attributes with a project plan in efforts

Deposit Your Dreams Into Success | "Dream, Desire, & Determination"

to list chronologically or sequentially for completions of task. The dreams become reality when you have the *Desire.*

Desire

Desire is the magic that makes everything happen! When you have desire, you have purpose, when you have purpose, you have vision! These are the tools for completing task and projects. It is very important to hold yourself accountable when completing your goals on time. Often, people will hire a business mentor or coach to assist them with their goals. Ultimately, it is up to the individual with a burning desire to make things come into a reality.

Determination

Determination is the back-bone of hard work and dedication in fulfilling your Dreams. This is also the key ingredient for success and a pathway to your destiny. An important key of determination is surrounding yourself around other determined individuals also known as **"Go Getters"**. The willingness and sacrifice to get the job done no matter the circumstances. These are my strategies for the ultimate prize of leadership and intentional living for authenticate connections.

Deposit Your Dreams Into Success | "Dream, Desire, & Determination"

The road to success comes with a great deal of responsibility; the irony of good deeds and having a good heart is not always good enough. Leading by example and setting strong family values are keys to a purpose driven life. Shirley Chisholm once said, "Service is the rent we pay for the privilege of living on this earth". This quote is meaningful as look at serving others. It also gently reminds us of responsibilities and consequences accompany that life. It's not all fun and games. This quote urges us to help others, like Jesus did, in order to pave the way through life. In today's terminology, we call that paying it forward or, as I like to say, praying it forward. Jesus spoke to the disciples in parables because of the unwillingness by the people to receive Jesus' message of the Kingdom. The truths of the Kingdom of God were heard by them but not understood. It was not because God was hiding the truth from them, but it is because they did not want to hear.

In 2017, the NAACP recognized me as one of the State of Maryland's top influencers for community service. It was a blessing and a testament to earn the NAACP President's Award alongside another servant leader, retired Maryland State Senator Barbara Mikulski. I have recognized that my daily walk is to serve others, especially through business, to inspire and support the community in which I live, and to be blessed to be a blessing to others through Servant Leadership. Life has not always been easy for me. I became a single parent at 30. I faced many challenges in the military and as a civilian worker dealing with racism. As a man of Faith, I began realizing that life is about helping others and glorifying the Kingdom of God. I re-married at 34 and now have five children, and I strive every day to prepare them for strenuous days ahead. "Education is the passport to the future, for tomorrow belongs to those who prepare for today" quoted by Malcolm X.

Deposit Your Dreams Into Success | "Dream, Desire, & Determination"

Dr. Larry White, Sr.

CEO & Founder of VIPeVENTS Concierge, LLC.

www.vipeventsconcierge.com

Tiffany Williams-Parra
Entrepreneur | Author | Fitness Guru

Don't "weight" for your wake-up call -

My Journey to Health and Healing.

Tiffany Parra is a Certified Life Coach, Fitness Trainer, Best-Selling Author and Owner of Phoenix Fitness Fanatics. Born and raised in Southern California to John H. Williams, Marine and 30 - year veteran of the Los Angeles County Sheriff's department and Eunice E Williams, retired Boeing Aircraft Structural

Don't "weight" for your wake-up call - *My Journey to Health and Healing*

Mechanic, taught Tiffany to have a strong work ethic and the drive to always push through.

After a major 100lb+ weight release, Tiffany found a strong desire to help others learn how to navigate through life's chaos in order to find that winning combination to create a long-lasting healthy lifestyle. Helping people find the drive to get started and keep going has been Tiffany's highest inspiration. Ensuring all the people she touches are healthier and happier is what gives her the passion to wake up every day. Working hard and pushing through adversity to achieve desired results reaps the best benefits. When we learn to rise above adversities, regardless of the situation, we see it is possible to conquer anything that comes your way!

The momentum to get started is the toughest struggle people have in any health and wellness journey. People find every excuse to not get into action. "I'm too busy." "I'm too tired." "I have no time." Any reason to get out of doing things to enhance their mind, body and spirit. Why is that? Is it Fear? Is it poor planning?

It's now time to embark on a journey to find that inner spark that will help you transform into the best version of you yet. Will it be hard? Yes! Will you be in pain sometimes? Yes! Will you be uncomfortable? Yes! Last, will it be worth it? Well, I will let you decide that for yourself, but my answer is YES!!!

Now, let me ask you something. Have you ever paid attention to the surrounding leaders? The CEO at the company who spends

Don't "weight" for your wake-up call - *My Journey to Health and Healing*

hours in meetings trying to figure it all out or the HR Manager ensuring all the employees are following the rules. No matter what the position, each one has one thing in common. Something that can make or break the person… And that is what I call the "Hamster wheel Syndrome". This is where you are moving so fast through the operation of your professional and/or personal life you forget the one thing which is the MOST important, your health. After years in HR Management, struggling to build a business I was passionate about, and trying to be the best mom I could be, I found myself stuck on that wheel. I would work 10–12 hours a day most days and skip meals to make sure I got to meetings on time. I smoked almost a pack of cigarettes a day just to cope with the stress, and exercise was not on my agenda.

In 2008, I found myself at a crossroads. I was at my heaviest weight ever, which was well over 200 pounds. To be honest, I weighed almost 300 pounds. I was told at a routine doctor appointment, I was prediabetic with extremely high blood pressure and bad cholesterol. When my sugar was tested, it was close to 280 while fasting. If you are familiar with sugar levels, you know we should be about 125 or below.

This was extremely disheartening and eye opening at the same time. I was a single working mom with a young son who was my main priority. But how could I take care of him if I were on the brink of some serious health issues? "This is not happening to me," is all I kept reciting in my head as I drove home from the appointment with tears rolling down my face.

Don't "weight" for your wake-up call - *My Journey to Health and Healing*

In the days to come, I felt depressed and defeated. So, I did what I was always told to do by my parents and grandparents. I prayed about it. I asked God to give me the wisdom to figure out how to fix this because I refused to go on any medications! I prayed for inner strength to help me make the right decisions in the journey I was about to take, and the courage to make the changes needed to succeed.

It was time to disrupt my normal routine, which was horrifying but necessary if I were to win this battle of getting my health back on track. There were so many things I needed to change, but I did not know where to start. I had to create healthy meals at home when it was so easy to hop on over to the cafeteria or walk to the surrounding restaurants.

Then I had to figure out how I was going to add in working out when I was already stretched thin with the long hours and my 2-3-hour commute home each day. You would think getting in a workout would be easy enough since we had a full-service gym on site where I worked. They even had showers and provided towels to get cleaned up. With all the wonderful amenities, I still tried to make every excuse why I could not go there.

One Friday evening, I was playing a game with my son. I observed him laughing and being his joyful self. I realized the changes I had to make were not just for me. They were for him as well. I needed to teach him how to be healthy so he could grow up fit and strong.

Don't "weight" for your wake-up call - *My Journey to Health and Healing*

On Monday I showed up to work with my workout clothes and tennis shoes in my backpack, ready to start my journey to better health. I was determined not to allow my busy lifestyle and unhealthy eating habits to affect my health any longer. I started with a few minutes on the treadmill or stairs, along with a little weight training.

Every day I showed up, I noticed the CEO of the company, along with a handful of other high-level executives working out in the gym as well. One day I even saw the top executive in Human Resources on the elliptical machine. I asked how often she worked out and she replied, "At least 5 days a week." That conversation really made me think. If she could workout daily with her hectic, crazy schedule, I know I can too! I hated hearing her talk on her phone when she worked out in the gym with us, but she was there, and that's what matters most.

After consistently working out for a couple of months, I had a surprising conversation with the CEO. He gave me praise on my progress and asked me why I got started in the gym. I told him about my diagnosis. He replied, "Well that's not a death sentence." I looked at him, a bit puzzled, as he continued. "When you are committed to staying in consistent action, you can change almost anything. Remember, this journey is yours, not anyone else's. You'll be just fine if you are true to yourself, have faith in your abilities and learn to be your own cheerleader." This was a game changer for me! I needed to learn to focus and celebrate myself through the journey.

Don't "weight" for your wake-up call - *My Journey to Health and Healing*

In the coming months, I adjusted my eating by doing weekly meal prep sessions on Sunday afternoons. I made them fun by playing my favorite music and throwing in a glass of wine. I started running at lunch in addition to my workout since I was saving 20-25 minutes just by meal prepping. I started signing up for 5k runs to challenge myself and found a passion for running which later led me to run the Long Beach marathon in 2015. In 6 months, I released almost 50 pounds and my blood sugar levels, blood pressure, and cholesterol were in normal ranges. I continued to work full-time hours but adjusted where I could. I added in 1–2 hours of working out each day, and I meditated and pray daily. I posted positive affirmations for weight loss on my mirror at home, on my desk at work, and in my car to help keep me accountable. Within 3 years I released well over 100 pounds and have maintained a healthy weight for almost a decade.

Stress is a silent killer. Taking control of your busy life by adding daily exercise and healthy eating is one of the best ways to prevent it. Through my journey, it has become my mission to help those struggling find a healthy work/life balance in their lives. In 2018, I launched my company, Phoenix Fitness Fanatics to help people create a well-balanced, healthy lifestyle they can thrive in and not just survive. I teach my clients how to find the momentum to keep going and help them establish mindfulness around their daily activity level and food choices. I use proven methods you probably have all heard but have never put in practice like being consistent or

Don't "weight" for your wake-up call - *My Journey to Health and Healing*

having an accountability partner. Using healthy affirmations and meditation are also daily practices that can help elevate your mind, body, and spirit. Incorporating these tools will help you create the ultimate healthy lifestyle change for years to come.

In my journey, they reminded me early on that it's all about having faith in yourself and your abilities. We get so caught up in our busy lives we forget to acknowledge the beautiful, brilliant human beings that we are. Celebrate yourself by taking a step back to assess your life. If you are not living a balanced, healthy lifestyle created to help you shine brightly in whatever it is you do, it's time for a change. Schedule a date to set everything else aside for a moment and focus on you. Focus on what you need to do to look and feel your best.

Creating a healthy lifestyle is the greatest gift you can give to yourself. It's self-care which we have found is a necessity, not just a choice.

Stop allowing work, home, school, and all the other distractions in your life impede you stepping into your power and purpose. You have been created to do some amazing things! If I can balance it all, I have full faith that you can too!

Now are you ready to get off your "Hamster Wheel" so you can focus on being the best version of yourself inside and out? Let me be your guide on that journey. It will not only be rewarding, but it could save your life.

To start on your journey to better health, connect with Coach Tiffany to book your Weight Release Strategy call today!

http://app.fitnessismylife.co.uk/tiffanyw/strategy/

Here's how you can find out more about Tiffany and join her amazing Fitness community on social media.

Website: http://app.fitnessismylife.co.uk/tiffanyw/

Instagram: https://www.instagram.com/coach_tiffanyparra/

Facebook Business Page: https://www.facebook.com/PFFCoachIT

Facebook Group Page: https://www.facebook.com/groups/373719946381942

Eric A. Lomax

Entrepreneur | Business Consultant

FISHER OF MEN

Eric Lomax is the CEO of the Lomax Consulting Team and the author of From Grief to Glory the Rise of the Centurion. He is also an ordained minister and has served many denominations, including Baptist, and the Church of God in Christ. He is passionate about leading men into their God given purpose. Eric

FISHER OF MEN

has served the church as an Assistant Pastor, Marriage Counselor, Deacon, and a Sunday School Superintendent.

Before embarking on his entrepreneurial career path, Eric worked for Delta Airlines as Customer Service Representative at the Detroit Metropolitan Airport. While at Delta Eric served as an ambassador on the Front-Line Involvement Team F.I.T., which was a liaison between management and employees. The purpose of F.I.T. was to help break down communication barriers and disseminate information that was pertinent to keeping the operation running smoothly. Prior to that, Eric spent many years in corporate America as a Sales Representative for various companies like Verizon Wireless, and Chase Bank where he honed his communication skills. Taking what he has learned in the trenches of corporate America, Eric has embarked on teaching those skills to individual and groups all over the world. He is an accomplished speaker, coach, and trainer that seeks to bring out the best in everyone.

Why can't men work together; and why can't we seem to trust one another? I know that this is a problem for men of all races, but I am speaking specifically to African American men. Black men are plagued with these faults and it has crippled us since our ancestors set foot on this land. Yes, the genocide known as

FISHER OF MEN

slavery handles the plight of the black man because that is where it all began. Black male slaves were hit with physical and mental abuse by slave owners that sought to keep them locked in the grips of slavery. And even though we have been set free physically, someone still trapped us within our minds from the seeds of discord that were sown long ago. The infamous and incendiary letter penned by Willie Lynch has kept our race from progressing in society to this day. In it he outlines the process to keep us from ever succeeding by sowing fear, envy, and distrust amongst the slaves. They instructed slave masters to place division and envy between young and old and dark-skinned and light-skinned slaves. These tactics were quite successful, and they have plagued our men to this very day. We are producing boys who no longer respect anything or anyone. And we are still unwilling to assist one another rise positions of power. Our envy of one another runs deep within in our souls.

FISHER OF MEN

Growing up as a light-skinned black male was a traumatic experience because I faced ridicule from racism and bullying from my people. I was not white enough to pass as white, and I was not black enough to be black. I was caught in the middle of trying to figure out where I belonged. My life was filled with constant threats and harassment from my own men, and I constantly tried to prove to them I was indeed black. I was often called white boy and asked if I was mixed. Whenever I walked into a room, I could feel the stares by those who mocked me for being light-skinned. But what they did not know is the fact that my light-skinned peers did not embrace me because I did not come from the same socio-economic background. My family had no prominence, and we did not belong to any of the upper-class social organizations like Jack and Jill. I came from a family of blue-collar workers who were raised in the plants. My father worked for and retired from the city as a sanitation supervisor and none of my brothers graduated from college. We were taught

FISHER OF MEN

to work hard with our hands, and they did not pressure us to attend college. They taught us to make our own way and not to expect help from anyone. Especially those that had the power to open doorways to success. In my neighborhood, it was every man for himself.

I believe we should all have mentors and aspire to mentor others. Jesus was the ultimate mentor to the disciples who followed him. As he stood on the shore watching the boats come in from a long night of fishing, he looked towards Peter and told him to follow and he would make him a fisher of men. The scriptures instruct us to care about our brothers and to help them grow. We can only do this by investing in one another. I believed in this so much that I made it a point to seek mentors to help me in my career pursuits; however, all I found were men who sought to hinder or deny my talent. I did not understand it, but the residual effects of the Willie Lynch letter were working in the background. I attended many networking events with other black men who had

FISHER OF MEN

risen through the ranks, hoping that they would take me under their wing and show me the path to success. However, all I received from them was the cliché phrase of my need to pull myself up by my own bootstraps. Or they totally forgot about me and all the other men who looked to them for guidance on how to make it into leadership positions. The lessons that I learned from them were that self-preservation was the only thing that mattered.

We can say the same of the black church. You would think that the church would understand God's plan to advance the kingdom, but they are following the ways of the world by denying good men from receiving the fruits of the kingdom. In most black churches across America, women disproportionately outnumber the men. Why is this happening today? Why do most men stay away from the church? I believe one reason is because churches do not have programs that help men grow and become better citizens within the community. Churches need to

FISHER OF MEN

understand that men are in crisis not only spiritually, but they also face crisis in their homes and in their jobs. The church needs to stop being concerned about itself and focus on the needs of the community it serves. Healthy communities depend on strong caring men who are foundational to its success. Think about it, if the church made it a priority to teach men how to be sons of God, we would have stronger families, stronger companies, and stronger governments because each man would be an example to other men. Men would compel other men to be and do better by looking out for one another. This would also give young men suitable role models to respect and emulate.

I was called to ministry back in 1995 at Allen Temple Baptist Church in Oakland, California, where I entered the Minister in Training Program. I felt the call to serve God and be a vessel of hope to all who were lost. However, my trajectory stalled in

FISHER OF MEN

many of the churches that I belonged to because I noticed the recurrent theme of mistrust, envy, and jealousy working within the hearts of many pastors that I served. It never deterred me from wanting to be a servant to the men that were supposed to help me become a pastor one day, but that help never came. From the time that I was ordained until now, I have faced the petty jealousies of insecure men. All I ever wanted to do was serve and be a servant to the men that I respected and admired, but none would encourage or help me rise within ministry. I became disappointed and disgusted with the politics within the church, and I noticed it set most ministries up as fiefdoms that were intent on retaining power. Family members were given key positions regardless of their qualifications, which meant that they denied capable men who could help grow the ministry. This nepotistic practice has destroyed many great ministries because the men in charge were only interested in themselves and not training up qualified successors. The church is supposed to train,

FISHER OF MEN

teach, and then send them to reach, but sadly this is not the case because some churches are being run by power hungry megalomaniacs masquerading as shepherds.

So, what solves this problem and how do we stem the tide of a system that keeps us enslaved? This is the mission of the Lomax Consulting Team, as we seek to be a resource for men to understand their purpose in the world and in their homes. My group seeks to train men with a wholistic approach to understanding their purpose in society and the family structure. We can achieve this in a corporate setting and one-on-one consultations. In the corporate setting, we can lead both small and large training group sessions that bridge gaps between employees and management, facilitating open and honest conversations that will spur trust and growth. We dissect the corporate culture and look for ways to improve

FISHER OF MEN

communication and overall employee satisfaction. Our priority is to create stronger leaders who focus on mentoring and training to prepare for future successions within the company. We geared our individual sessions towards doing deep dives into a client's personal life to pinpoint and target the areas that hinder growth. Our goal is to destroy negative mindsets that are hindrances to growth and accountability.

Our consultation packages for ministries focus on the succession plan of the pastor and the programs that are geared towards men. Succession plans are key in all areas of the church, including Deacons, trustees, and the heads of all affiliate ministries within the church. This will ensure the longevity of the ministry and ease the destruction that power struggles bring. We also review and design programs for men and plan strategies to attract and retain strong men who are leaders in their communities, companies, and their homes. My goal is to make sure that men

FISHER OF MEN

work together to destroy the negative DNA of jealousy, envy, and fear that has plagued us for far too long.

The Lomax Consulting Team is available for speaking engagements in both the corporate and spiritual settings. To inquire about bookings, please contact Eric Lomax at (313) 903-3742, or www.lomaxconsultingteam.com, or

elomax524@gmail.com

Demetrica "Meechie" Jefferis
Military Veteran | Entrepreneur | Financial Expert

Breaking Through Traditional Thinking: Shifting Mindsets for Financial Greatness

A Chicago native, Air Force Retiree, Breast Cancer Survivor, and author of "No More Bad Days", Mrs. Jefferis is a licensed Financial Services Agent. Since receiving her license in Sept 2018, she has financially educated and empowered hundreds of Americans to make, save, grow, and protect their money. She has also helped families and businesses across the U.S. secure nearly $7.5M in wealth and financial protection. Meechie continues to

Breaking Through Traditional Thinking: Shifting Mindsets for Financial Greatness

spread the importance of financial literacy within educational institutions, non-profit organizations, religious establishments, and support groups. Her liberating message can also be heard through social media channels and social business networks.

"Compound interest is the eighth wonder of the world. He who understands it, earns it…He who doesn't…pays it." Albert Einstein.

"How many of you have heard of the Rule of 72?" In July 2018, at a Business Presentation Meeting, someone asked me this question. While they spoke it in English, the concept was foreign to me. "The rule of who?", I asked. At 47 years of age, I am exposed to a basic financial principle so simple, yet so powerful. As the instructor took his time explaining this rule, I couldn't help but quietly ask myself:

"Why haven't I heard of this before?"

"How have I been getting through life without knowing and practicing this golden rule?"

"How could I have served 26 years in uniform and never learn about this?"

There's an answer to these questions: Traditional thinking. I grew up watching my parents work hard. And most of my friends' parents did the same thing. No one ever talked about owning their own business or learning how to do better with their savings. The only thing my parents knew is what they shared: 1. Get an education; 2. Get a job; 3. Save your money… Besides

Breaking Through Traditional Thinking: Shifting Mindsets for Financial Greatness

family, there was nothing existing outside of that. Naturally, I learned to work hard. And saving my money meant opening a savings account. My parents did not teach me about the Rule of 72. All they knew was to work hard, and work harder, to provide for their family, and never consider retirement, or building a legacy of wealth. Instead, they worked themselves sick and died without leaving a financial legacy for their children to prosper and continue to build up in their honor. This repetitive cycle of working hard for someone else's agenda, being comfortable with debt, never learning how money works, and doing better with money becomes the legacy.

For most of my adult life, I was a product of traditional thinking. However, when I learned about the Rule of 72, there was an immediate shift in mindset. I wanted to learn more. I wanted to change my attitude towards money. Especially seeing there is more beyond checking, savings, and a 401K or TSP. At that moment, I stripped away the traditional thinking of "I got my pension, VA Disability, and my husband's military pension and income…I'm good!" Traditional thinking for many years made me believe the military would take care of me. There's no need for me to seek other forms of life protection. I have the SGLI. I have benefits. I'm comfortable. What more is there? When I shifted my mindset, I listened and learn the hidden treasures of how to build wealth; and it did not take long to see there is so much more.

Breaking Through Traditional Thinking: Shifting Mindsets for Financial Greatness

The shift allowed me to clearly see that something trapped me in a traditional mindset that my parents were trapped in. They only knew how to work for someone else and accept what was given. They never learned how to double their money over time (the basic principle of the Rule of 72).

For 26 years, I was that person. Everything my employer told me was gold. What I realized is that my employer only told me what it wanted me to know. Sadly, millions of people,

government and military professionals included only know what their employer tells them. And because of the traditional mindset, not only are they close-minded to learning from other trusted outside sources, TIME is wasted. Time is a valuable asset we can never recoup. Especially for money. Even now, I carry a huge regret for not being more aggressive in seeking out knowledge to build wealth. 26 years of doubling money over time—gone.

After attending weekly financial workshops, and learning more about money than I ever imagined, it convicted me to take a leap of faith in Sept 2018 and paved a career path as a licensed Financial Services Agent. Not only did I shift into building a solid financial foundation for my family, I also wanted to share this with others. Surely, I was not the only 47-year-old who was completely ignorant to the Rule of 72, amongst other financial principles. Traditional thinking pushed on us by society encourages us to accept debt as a way of life. But I was a 47-year-old ready to take control of my finances, learn more, and do better. And I did. Now I am putting the Rule of 72 to work FOR me instead of AGAINST me. And for the first time in my life, I

Breaking Through Traditional Thinking: Shifting Mindsets for Financial Greatness

am uncomfortable with debt and no longer accept it. I am watching my money double before my eyes. And I was especially ready to help others eradicate traditional thinking about money and experience even greater joys of financial freedom.

So, what does it take to shift your mind towards financial greatness?

1. An open mind. One of the major downfalls to reaping financial greatness is a narrowminded view. As I mentioned before, whatever my former employer told me was enough. After all, I was in a sheltered environment, overflowing with benefits. And since I led a comfortable lifestyle, I believed that was it and nothing more. But once I saw some of those benefits, "like good old" SGLI taken from me, and now I had to search for my own life insurance, I was completely lost. I knew nothing about life insurance. And because I opened my mind to receive financial knowledge, I discovered how terribly ignorant I was about money.
2. Application of knowledge. I saw the power of what was being taught at the workshops. I could even share what I had learned with others. But knowing is not enough. Application is critical of change. Financial greatness requires change. For a solid decade I kept telling myself I want to learn about money. And when I got the chance, I hesitated on applying what I learned. A promotion doesn't happen without application of skills. And you certainly wouldn't select a doctor to operate on you without knowing he/she has applied what he/she learned.

Breaking Through Traditional Thinking: Shifting Mindsets for Financial Greatness

3. So, what was I waiting for? I had already wasted 28 years on financial waste. I needed to do something different.
4. Courage… COURAGE. Traditional thinking gives us a sense of comfort and security in spaces of familiarity. But nothing can grow or change there. Your family and friends live there with you. When you receive truth, your mind challenges you to break free from that space you've been living in far too long. To do better, exercise courage to break free from that space of traditional thinking. Some of your influences in that space will applaud you, support you, take the journey to financial greatness with you, and others will either distance themselves from you, mock you, or downright disown you. When I embarked on my journey to financial greatness as my money manager and licensed Financial Services Agent, family and friends removed themselves from my space. One powerful lesson here: It will hurt, but not for long. Everyone cannot ride along. So be prepared to love them in their space and prosper in yours.

Are you ready to shift into financial greatness? Recognize you can always learn more about money and do better at any AGE. I was 47 when I started learning about money, debt management principles, and establishing wealth. In less than 3 years, I established my financial business, have gained superb control of my money, and working towards other financial goals. I challenge you to open your mind to establishing financial greatness in your life right now. With an open mind, application of knowledge, and courage, you can build a legacy of wealth, and tear down the traditional thinking walls of debt and poverty.

R. Wesley Webb
Bestselling Author | Visionary Author

R. Wesley Webb, MBA, MS

Mr. Wesley Webb is a federal employee with Homeland Security. His career spans numerous federal agencies in the District of Columbia (DC) metropolitan area and Europe.

Mr. Webb is an Army veteran that served 5 ½ years at the Landstuhl Regional Medical Center in Germany. While serving in Germany, he deployed to Saudi Arabia in support of Operation Desert Storm/Shield, and was awarded the Southwest Asia Service Medal with two bronze stars and the Kuwaiti Liberation Medal.

Mr. Webb is dedicated to serving his community; he currently serves as the President of the 100 Black Men of Maryland and on the National Board of the 100 Black Men of America. Through his leadership he stabilized the organization and position the Chapter for growth by increasing the number of financial members and enforcing minimum service hour requirements.

Mr. Webb is a member of Phi Beta Sigma Fraternity Inc. and is affiliated with the Tri-Sigma Graduate Chapter in Montgomery County MD. He led in the creation of the Taylor, Morse & Brown Foundation and served as the Foundation's first President in supporting the Chapter's charitable activities in the community.

Mr. Webb completed a dual master's program in Business Administration and Sustain Base Leadership from the University of Maryland University College, Adelphi, MD. He also received a Bachelor of Science in Criminal Justice from the University of Maryland University College's European Division located in Heidelberg Germany.

Mr. Webb is a contributing author in the best-selling book, "When Men Lean In, We All Win" which was published in 2020. He grew up in Marion, IN and currently lives in Silver Spring, MD with his wife, Mechelle D. Johnson-Webb, Esq.

Wise Counsel

The value of wise counsel is worth its weight in gold when applying experiences in life to the way we learn. I will share my perspective on this matter coupled with experiences from my own life and reflected upon the self-help guru Napoleon Hill's motivating factor of desire.

Although, first let's focus on learning. When you think about the process of "learning," you immediately connect it to the idea of thinking. Therefore, if you can conceive it you can achieve it! We are the product of our thoughts and it is important to be careful in what we consciously internalize. The reason I say this is because learning entails engaging your complete personality, including your senses, feelings, intuition, beliefs, values, and will. Once you begin learning about something, whatever you feed to your brain, impacts your personality and behavior.

Recent research has confirmed that learning is a continuous process that starts at birth and continues till death. It is how we use our experience to deal with new situations and develop relationships. Almost every action we take is the result of past learning. Learning is fundamental and can be distinguished in four stages, which are:

- Unconscious incompetence - we are unaware of our lack of knowledge and understanding.
- Conscious Incompetence - we are aware of our lack of knowledge and understanding.
- Conscious Competence - we make an effort to increase our level of knowledge and understanding.

- Unconscious Competence   - we don't have to ponder about knowing it, as somewhere in our subconscious mind, we already know it.

We must first 'desire' to learn and Napoleon Hill begins with desire as the catalyst for success. Many people want to be successful, but merely wanting success is a waste of time as it just produces frustration. Only a burning, all-consuming, enthusiastic, and passionate desire will produce exceptional results that make up true success.

Wanting is best understood by its second meaning in the dictionary, which is "to lack." To want something is to lack something, and so long as you merely want success, you will lack it. Want is similar to wishful thinking, while desire, on the other hand, is an extremely potent force. It is a supreme motivator and an abstract principle of creation. Desire is an energetic emanation of the human spirit that enacts the law of attraction. Desire is the metaphysical equivalent of gravity as it draws you toward what you want, or the elements that will constitute the thing desired. Desire is the fuel that ignites the fire that transforms thoughts into reality. The sad truth about most people who claim to want success is that they actually do not desire it.

The last two stages of the learning process is where I intend to focus. I possess the desire and will to learn and use that knowledge to understand how I can achieve success in different areas of my life. Moreover, I tend to surround myself with individuals that challenge and help me grow personally, which is

Wise Counsel

the true essence of the philosophy of iron sharpens iron in which the Signature Entrepreneurs & Mastermind group supports.

I was born with the desire to learn and succeed. However, my desire to improve was cultivated by recurring opportunities that I had for seeking advice on how to fulfill these desires. Advice is an integral part of growing, improving, and achieving your dreams. You must weigh the value of the advice you receive by familiarizing yourself with the source, what their experience level is, and whether it can help you do better. Knowledge is a gift which will serve you well in the game of life if you can learn how to apply it properly.

Napoleon Hill goes to great lengths to make the distinction between generalized knowledge and specialized knowledge, which is another one of his secrets to success. He cited examples of the lives of certain individuals in an offhanded manner to shed light on the most important things about knowledge. Here, it's plainly spoken knowledge, by and of itself, has little, if any, value. You may find that shocking, or at least contrary, to everything you've learned in the past, but it is true. Knowledge only becomes valuable in its application. You may have heard that knowledge is power. That isn't entirely wrong, but it is incomplete. It is applied knowledge that begets power, wealth, and the advancement of humanity. The secret is in the application, not in knowledge itself.

I appreciate the advice that I received early on in life, and it increased more as I grew into an adult. I began my life in a comfortable environment and my parents worked hard to afford a middle-class lifestyle for me and my brothers. The lessons that my

Wise Counsel

parents instilled in us laid the foundation for understanding the value of hard work and not second guessing our capabilities when things got tough.

During my childhood, I spent a lot of time with my grandfather, Moses Webb Sr. He was a hardworking man who wasn't in the habit of tolerating any nonsense and one of the smartest individuals I know, despite only attending school to the fourth grade so he could help his father with work on the farm. My grandfather spent his formative years working with his father to ensure they had a successful harvest each season. Farming continued to be a part of his life even after he left the south and started working in the blue-collar industry.

He knew the value of a dollar and applied that knowledge in his life when he built his own house, he acquired land, and purchased other rental properties. The example he set for me, helped instill a strong work ethic. He taught me that in order to achieve something, you had to compromise on something else. The conversations I had with my grandfather were always quite enlightening, and the one saying that always stuck in my mind was, "You cannot get something for nothing." In other words, there is always going to be a tradeoff or an opportunity cost for whatever you want out of life, and this perhaps was the most valuable lesson that I learned from him at an early age.

My grandfather had a group of five veteran outpatients from the VA that lived in his house. I remember fondly naming this group of absolutely wonderful men as, "The Council of Elders" because they served as my personal advisors throughout my childhood. They advised me through my formative years and

Wise Counsel

placed great emphasis upon the value of common sense, which helped to instill a great deal of confidence.

I have always gravitated to seeking advice from those that were older than me because their advice seemed to be more reliable. I often compared the Council of Elders to the men in an African village. I truly respected the men; not simply because of their age and experience, but because of the lessons that I learned from them.

The Council also taught me the value of time and how a certain part of it should be spent on just thinking about various things, such as what you want out of life, where you would like to live if given the opportunity to move, and how you plan on earning a living in the future. Discovering the answers to these questions enabled me to form a blueprint that helped me build a foundation for my life that would not have been possible without the wise counsel of the Elders.

They provided me with one piece of advice that served me well in life which was the characteristics of a good man. They are:

1. Being a gentleman with good manners and etiquette
2. Being direct
3. Being faithful
4. Possessing integrity
5. Being honest
6. Displaying maturity
7. Possessing a strong sense of self-confidence
8. Nurturing a positive attitude

Wise Counsel

This particular piece of advice aided me while in college, and even when I joined the Army. I later learned how all of these characteristics are connected in helping you become the best version of yourself. For example, due to my faith and a strong sense of confidence I've always maintained a positive outlook on life. As a result, wherever I landed in life, I knew that I possessed the power to get back up and keep moving ahead if I failed at something.

I attribute my drive and spirit for life to three men in particular who I'm immensely grateful to, they are:

Moses Webb Sr. (Grandfather) – My grandfather was instrumental in instilling a strong sense of confidence in me. He equipped me with a strong work ethic and provided insight to individual character traits that insulated me against self-doubt.

Moses Webb Jr. (Father) – My father often reminded me that we all have the same amount of time in a day to accomplish our goals and, as a black man, I had to be three times as productive to make it in life. The discussions that we had help to fuel my drive for personal success. If you truly want to make it in life, you have to put in the hard work to achieve your goals. As a result, I'm continuously pushing myself to do better.

Charles Broussard (Step-Father) – My step-father struck the right balance as a role model by allowing me to be completely free, to just be myself. He introduced me to Jazz, and we shared a love for Miles Davis. I often listen to, "Kind of Blue and Bitches Brew" which exposed me to the culture of cool music. Miles had

Wise Counsel

a keen sense of style and I found myself reading GQ to create my own look.

I left for college in the Fall of 1984 after I graduated from high school and began my undergraduate studies at Vincennes University. The lessons I learned prepared me for the next phase of my life without a parental safety net. The campus life was a microcosm of the real world where I could experiment with different viewpoints and engage my peers in debating complex issues concerning race, interracial relationships, sex, and politics. The experience was quite enlightening and helped me discover a few things about myself as I continued to pursue my studies.

I graduated from the Vincennes University in the Spring of 1986 with an associate degree in Marketing and an attitude that spoke volumes about how I was ready to take on the world. However, as fate would have it, the local businesses weren't prepared to hire again due to the recession and as a consequence the economy was quite weak. As a result, I decided to join the Army in the winter of 1986, after consulting with my stepfather, who had served in Vietnam. The advice he provided helped me to make a life changing decision with confidence. There is always an emotional, financial, or social cost associated with any significant decision to be made, which is why having access to reliable friends or family members who you can consult in such a situation is critical to success.

Afterward, I headed off to Fort Jackson, SC, where I would receive basic training. Initially, the training itself was extremely challenging in every sense of the word. I felt like I was in a particularly vulnerable position because I was further away than I

Wise Counsel

had ever been from everything I had always considered normal. However, after a couple of weeks, I began to adapt to the routine of the classroom instruction and the physical rigors of training.

I am very grateful that I remained emotionally grounded because if I hadn't been, I would have lost my way like so many others. Whenever times got tough, I always remembered my grandfather's saying, "You cannot get something for nothing." As I reflect upon this point, I realize that my upbringing prepared me well for life and equipped me with the mental fortitude to persevere. I completed my basic training in the Spring of 1987 and was assigned to Landstuhl Regional Medical Center, in Landstuhl Germany.

Working at the medical command in Landstuhl was an exciting period in my life. The military community where I resided had the largest concentration of Americans outside the US. The Germans I encountered, or lived amongst, were very accommodating to Americans in their country. I immersed myself in the culture by frequenting the restaurants, learning their language, dating, and driving fast cars on the autobahn.

I also consider myself fortunate for being able to meet several good people who always provided me with excellent advice. I'd be a remiss if I didn't recognize some of those individuals that helped me along the way.

Therefore, I would like to pay a tribute to:

- Colonel Jesse Nason

Wise Counsel

Jesse was a Quartermaster Army officer; he and I shared an affiliation through the Phi Beta Sigma fraternity. He always looked out for me in ways that I couldn't have anticipated back then. I think he knew that I had other ambitions and that the Army was not for me personally, but felt that he could give me a helping hand by being a great mentor.

- CW4 Joe Lofton:

Joe was funny, I honestly never had a dull moment with him. He taught me not to take life so seriously and learn to laugh more. As he often pointed out, there is always someone who is not as fortunate, and I should be counting my blessings daily. He left a real impact on my life and taught me to be grateful for every little thing.

- SFC William (Will) Bass:

Will was the epitome of cool; he always had a good-looking woman with him. He helped me to ease into being more sociable. He taught me the art of small talk which helped me to open up more and assisted me in overcoming some of my short comings.

It was indeed a privilege to serve with all of them, and I wouldn't have traded the experience for the world. However, like all good things change crept in rather quickly as I got selected for a deployment in support of Operation Desert Storm/Shield in the winter of 1989. I recall feeling a rush of angst within me since I would not be able to see my family before I left. I believe that was perhaps one of the lowest points in my life, but I did manage to keep a positive outlook on things despite the circumstances I was forced to confront.

Wise Counsel

I re-deployed in the Spring of 1990 back to Landstuhl Germany and was focused on getting out of the Army within two years. As a result, I started planning and committing to some goals that I'd written down while deployed to help me stay focused.

I was assigned to the medical logistics distribution operations where I met Captain (CPT) Kelvin Smart, and completed the remaining time of my tour in Germany. As I prepared to leave the Army in the Spring of 1992, CPT Smart offered me an entry level government position. I was absolutely elated at the opportunity to stay in country and work. However, before doing so, I needed to consult with my family back in the States. I finished processing out of the Army and returned the US to see my family. I remained in the states for six months and received my parents blessing before returning to Germany to work.

Cpt. Smart and I stayed in touch with one another while I was in the states. He was essential in helping me to plot my future and accomplish two of my primary goals which were to:

- Obtain government job
- Complete my bachelor's degree

The decision to get out of the Army served me well and I attribute that to the goals that I had set for myself.

As Napoleon Hill says, the ability to make firm, clear, and resolute decisions is as precious a gift as life itself. It is what enables us as human beings to take control of our lives, to rise above chance and circumstance, and to chart our own destiny. As result, the decisions that we make today will determine our circumstances for tomorrow therefore, do so wisely.

Gina Goree Hitchens RICP®

Retirement Income Certified Professional Planner

Speaker | Trainer | Financial Planner and Coach

SMART Women Finish Strong

"Start Strong | Stay Strong | Finish Strong"

SMART Women Finish Strong
"Start Strong | Stay Strong | Finish Strong"

As a Financial Planner, with 30+ years of industry experience, in a male dominated industry, Gina is passionate about one thing- using her unique voice to transform the financial lives of women and their families.

In 2008, her unique vision and desire to help women achieve a more Purposeful Life~ drove Gina to make an ambitious decision to leave her former firm and open GHG Financial Planning. A full-service independent advisory firm that allows her to offer her clients more through a personalized, 1:1 approach. Gina is fully licensed to offer Insurance, Investments and Financial Planning Products and Services.

Gina is a Certified Speaker | Trainer | Facilitator and Coach with the John Maxwell International Team.

Being a woman with many years of life lessons, I appreciate the importance of being surrounded by a *Circle of "SMART Women"* - women with enough life experience to realize what in life is most important. I value their wit, wisdom, inspiration, and courage.

Many of these women have spent their entire life wearing and juggling multiple hats and titles: Daughter, Sister, Wife, and Mother- all while navigating the business and professional world as a working woman. I have worn and juggled them all, and now many of these titles are mere memories.

SMART Women Finish Strong
"Start Strong | Stay Strong | Finish Strong"

Over time, our day-to-day responsibilities lessen. At one point we juggled the responsibilities and joys of caring for husbands, raising children and sometimes being primary caregivers to aging parents. We now find ourselves empty nesters or rapidly approaching an empty nest and we are no longer blessed with living parents. During these *Seasons of Change,* we long to re-connect with *Self!*

The woman in the mirror.

Over the course of my life, I always recognized and stayed connected to my **Vision, Purpose and Passion,** but in all transparency, I did not always operate at peak performance. *What stopped me?*

I would often have quiet conversations with my 12-year-old self, and wonder who exactly is Gina? What does she want? What Inspires her? Frankly, I wanted to become fully re-engaged and connected with "The Woman in the Mirror."

Reflections and lessons learned.

During my seasons of transition, I recognized the importance of being Tribal- I realized I prospered and grew when I was surrounded by like-minded individuals. People of Value who sought to add Value to others.

As I navigate this journey called "Life" I recognized the importance of being surrounded by a Circle of SMART Women.

SMART Women Finish Strong

"Start Strong | Stay Strong | Finish Strong"

Women who readily recognize, understand, and appreciates the significance of Proverbs 27:17.

"Changing and Empowering the World One SMART Woman at a Time."

Who is in your circle?

It is often said that we become like the people we spend the most time with. I say, choose wisely,

So, I ask you, Who is in your circle? And what are they inspiring you to Become?

Your "Circle" should include SMART Women who are courageous enough to use their unique voice to **Encourage**, **Equip** and **Empower** others. towards success. Women who have a Vision, Purpose and Calling that is bigger than themselves.

"We Must Lift as We Climb."

By now, you are probably wondering who exactly is a SMART Woman, and what fuels her Purpose and Passion! She is:

Success Oriented Seeking to live a life of Significance.

Motivated with a Mature Mindset

SMART Women Finish Strong

"Start Strong | Stay Strong | Finish Strong"

Action oriented- and Authentic

Resourceful and Resilient- Uses her time and Resources to support her community.

Tried- Tested and Tribal.

This SMART Woman has a Heart and Soul for her family and her community. After all, remember, quite often is a Daughter, Sister, Wife, and Mother. She realizes that Success happens to you and Significance happens through you.

Back to the "Woman in the Mirror"

In becoming reconnected with self, the SMART Woman is not afraid to take an inward journey

of reflection and self-discovery. She must learn to "Be Still." On this journey, she must become intentional about identifying what is **REAL** to her. She must:

Realize her gifts, purpose, and passion.
Embrace her calling and act.
"Changing and Empowering the World One SMART Woman at a Time."

SMART Women Finish Strong

"Start Strong | Stay Strong | Finish Strong"

Always show up and bring her true Authentic Self.

Live her truth - Listen to her inner voice- Lean in- Learn and Lead.
So now, I have one question? Are you a *SMART Woman*? Have you taken the time to take an inward journey of self-rediscovery? Three questions to guide you along your journey:

1. What do you want?
2. What fuels your purpose?
3. What stands in your way?

"What and Who Inspires You?"

My what.

As a Financial Planner, with 30+ years of industry experience, in a male dominated industry, I have met countless numbers of business and professional women, These, women enjoyed family and career success, and did all the things that "Good Girls" were taught to do.

In many aspects of life, they were accomplished and confident women... but *Financially Speaking, Not So Confident*. This concerned me because I knew these were accomplished women.

Then I soon realized these women were accomplished in their areas of expertise. Which leads us back to the need to be surrounded by a Circle of SMART Women. A community of women and men with varying gifts and calling- but with the same Purpose- People of Value who add Value to others.

"Transforming the Financial Lives of Woman"

A financially empowered woman financially empowers her family and her community. She doesn't keep a secret! Therefore, I am passionate about one thing~ using my unique voice to transform the financial lives of women.

As a financial professional, it is my vision that every woman will live a life of her design-
create wealth- and use her wealth to fulfill her dreams, enjoy her passions, expand her interests and leave a significant impact on her family and community.

"Wealth Is the Ability to Fully Experience Life," - Henry David Thoreau

My why.

"Changing and Empowering the World One SMART Woman at a Time."

After my 30+ years of marriage ended in divorce, I found myself Suddenly Single, and solely responsible for my own financial livelihood! In all transparency, a sense of financial insecurity overwhelmed me.

Luckily, I was Tribal, and my inner circle of Sister/Friends reminded me I was a *SMART Woman* and that SMART Women Finish Strong. My Sisters were there to **Encourage, Empower**

SMART Women Finish Strong

"Start Strong | Stay Strong | Finish Strong"

and Inspire me to embrace the principles of a *SMART Woman*.

Barriers to growth.

In embracing the principles of a SMART Woman, I needed to reflect on not only what motivates and inspires me but also on what were my barriers to growth. It did not take long to realize that my financial insecurities of adjusting to operating as Solo Gina prevented me from walking with Power and Purpose.

Money is not everything, but for enhancing the quality of life, it is crucial.

"The barrier to bold choices is not fear- it's money."

Again, I ask, "Are you a SMART Woman? Would you like to become a SMART Woman? Or guide and direct another Sister to become one?" If so, preparation is key.

Prepare to Pivot with a Plan

While getting my financial house in order, I had to embrace the principles of *Iron Sharpens Iron* and surround myself with success-oriented people who were also striving to live *Purpose Driven* lives. People that shared their gifts, talents, and resources to enrich the lives of others. I call this my "Success Circle".

SMART Women Finish Strong

"Start Strong | Stay Strong | Finish Strong"

From engagements with my *Success Circle*, I realized my story was not just for me- but to share- I needed to use my unique voice and story to inspire others.

What did I want?
One of the greatest gifts I want to leave my family is a *Life Well Lived*. I want to pass down the awareness of the need and the methods for creating and building long-term wealth and financial security. I want my legacy defined by Dignity, Independence, and Choice,

> **"Changing and Empowering the World One SMART Woman at a Time."**

What did I have to do?
After my divorce, I found myself on a relentless journey to rebuild my financial security. I was always aware of the need to *"Be Still"*, but I was on a mission. I had things I wanted to get done. I did not have time to stop!

> *"Push to Purpose"*
> Be still.
> Then out of nowhere March 2020 appeared, and like everyone else, I was *"Forced to Be Still."*
> New friends entered my life and *Challenged* me to "BE Still."
> I was told, "Gina, you are doing too much!" With little

SMART Women Finish Strong

"Start Strong | Stay Strong | Finish Strong"

choice, I stilled myself.
SMART Women Finish Strong
"Start Strong | Stay Strong | Finish Strong"

"My Quarantine Inward Journey"
Birth of a vision.
During my quietness, I became Empowered to operate on a higher level of my calling and was
inspired to launch *SMART Women Finish Strong*, a Financial and Empowerment Community for Women by Women.

A circle of Success Oriented women with the shared Vision and Purpose of using their unique voice to ***Empower, Encourage and Inspire*** other women towards success.

A collaborative and friendly environment where SMART Women share their inspiring stories of resilience, faith, and courage. Stories and voices that equip the "Whole Woman" with the confidence, tips, tools, strategies, and life lessons learned that propel them to *Finish Strong.*

Iron Sharpens Iron
Start Strong | Stay Strong | Finish Strong.

So, by now, you are probably asking, how to I prepare for a Strong Finish.

SMART Women Finish Strong

"Start Strong | Stay Strong | Finish Strong"

We need to become educated and confident in our ability to pass on valuable information, resources, and life lessons learned to the next generation. The best advice we can give our daughters and granddaughters is to plan early and not to depend on others for financial security.

Stay connected with Purpose. Keep the Faith. Be Still and know
Iron Sharpens Iron.

"Changing and Empowering the World One SMART Woman at a Time."

Gina Goree Hitchens, RICP®, MBA
Speaker | Trainer | Financial Planner and Coach
www.GHGFinancialPlanning.com

Start Strong | Stay Strong | Finish Strong.

Lisa Jones Harwell
Visionary Author | Publisher

Reinvented by His Design

Lisa Harwell is the founder and CEO of Redbaby Publishing, Inc, an independent consulting firm that specializes in ghost writing, editing, marketing and book publications. Writing under the pen name of Jones Harwell, she has written two suspense novels and is the visionary and host behind the podcast and media platform, Journeys with Jones Harwell.

Professionally, Mrs. Harwell spent over thirty years working in telecommunications as a customer service manager, and voice engineer responsible for managing voice services platforms for the Department of Labor, State Department, Price Waterhouse and Cooper, and Georgetown University. Other adjuncts from her illustrious career include project management, trainer and voice announcer.

Currently, Mrs. Harwell serves on the board of directors for the 3 C's of Trinity and Advocate 4 History, and previously served as administrator/registrar for two youth organizations specializing in sports and academics.

Mrs. Harwell holds a graduate degree in Early Childhood Studies specializing in Administration, Leadership and Management from Walden University. She received her undergraduate degree in Communication Studies from the University of Maryland University College (UMUC). Mrs. Harwell is also a member of Sigma Gamma Rho Sorority.

Lisa currently lives in Maryland with her husband Avery of twenty years. They have two children, Aleah and JeLan, and three grandchildren, Kaleo, Jaelah and Jayden.

Reinvented by His Design

What do you do in the middle of a pandemic when you have stepped out on faith to finally do what God has instructed you to do, your purpose, your passion? In late 2019, when I found out I had to have major surgery in November, God spoke to me and said in January 2020, I need for you to walk away from a career that I had been in for over 30 years. On and off through the years I would listen, and I would turn him off, but this was a confirmation that had been brewing for a few years. He always has a way of bringing you back to His point. I was tired; I was rundown and figured I would take a five-month sabbatical and then go back to work. Well, January came around and for the first time since graduating from high school in 1980, I would have a vacation break longer than the eight weeks I was out on maternity leave with my son back in 2003. In March, the pandemic hit, and the world paused. In May, I am thinking I would return to work by September; I began applying for jobs. Well, it's now the beginning of 2021, and I am still unemployed. I find myself in the same predicament as millions of other Americans right now. Times right now may look bleak, so what do I do, how do I stay encouraged? I do what I've always done since I was twenty years old. I stand on the promise I made to myself: spirit, truth and resilience. I stand on the shoulders of the matriarchs of my family, my mother, my bonus mother, my grandmothers. I promised myself that I would trust my spirit; that my spirit would never break. I promised to always speak my truth with grace and conviction. And I promised myself that no matter what, I would walk in my resilience.

My goal was to go to college and become a journalist. I wanted to be one behind the scenes. I wanted to tell the stories

Reinvented by His Design

that matter to people that showed the human spirit, that showed the human heart; their trials and tribulations, and how they overcome. Well, I got side-tracked. I had doubts about this gift God gave me. Serious doubts. Who would want to hear my stories, hear me speak? Our God is so patient. Every so often He would point me in the right direction, and I would turn left again.

     I started my career as a job order clerk, working for the Department of Army at Fort Rucker, AL as a civilian employee. Through perseverance, I ended up moving to Washington DC in the mid-1980s. When I started out my career in telecommunications, I didn't have a clue to what I was doing. I was a GS-5 secretary. I went to an interview to become a computer operator. It was a panel interview and the gentleman who eventually hired me his posed a question, "What does communication studies have to do with information technology?" I was attending college part time. Nervous, I spoke the first thing that came out of my mouth, which I rarely do, and it was simply "the hell if I know." I paused. At that moment it occurred to me I just lost this job. There is no way I'm going to get this position now. I was wrong. He liked my spunk, and I got hired. My shift was second shift, from four to eleven in the evening. When I came in, they had already completed most of the work for the day. It left me to do secretarial work. Mind you, they hired me to become a computer operator. I began coming to work at two hours early, following the team to learn what they were doing. One day I came in early and he asked me to draft a letter and again my mouth had a "truth moment." I told him, "You did not hire me to be a secretary, you hired me to be a computer tech." It was that confidence that led me to be offered another position

Reinvented by His Design

with him at Georgetown University, to build the infrastructure for their first in-house voice and data services team.

Again, I knew nothing about building phone systems. I am working with engineers and for the first few months; I am drowning. None of the terminology is sticking and for the first time in my career, I am questioning myself about did I have the moral fiber for this position. One Friday, I had a meeting with my direct manager. It was brutal, and I cried, in front of the manager (another no-no). I went home that weekend feeling deflated. But God reminded me of my promise to me. I dusted myself off, looked in the mirror and stated, "you are going to float until you make it." Many of you might have heard that saying "sink or swim." I dog paddled for another year, then I swam. My determination, the resilience in me to keep moving to learn something to better myself, was my power. But I still didn't have the faith or courage for what God really intended for me to do. See, we can be anything, but can we do what God has designed for us to be?

My spirit is my faith; what I lean on, what I count and depend on when times are great and when times get stressful. I always know that I can go and talk to my God and he will be there for me. Now when I talk about my truth, these are the things I care most about, family, my inner circle, community issues. One is literacy. We cannot give up on our children's ability to read and comprehend. The ability to read and comprehend hinges on everything we attempt to accomplish in life. I come from kings and queens. I refuse to let someone take away my ability and right to learn. We must continue to fight for

Reinvented by His Design

the generations that come behind us. That is my truth. My resilience is simply that I cannot give up. I will not give up. My matriarchs fought for my right to be here. For my right to breathe. For my right to walk, contribute and aspire and inspire, not only me but others to find their purpose, their passion and be great at it. That is resilience and we are a resilient people.

In July 2019, I published my first novel. My intent was to take the novel to a friend of mine who has her own publishing company. She told me once I finished, she would publish it for me. When I finally finished the novel and it was ready for publication, she said to me, "Lisa you have all the tools to do this yourself". In my mind I was simply just going to self-publish and that was going to be the end. But God in his infinite wisdom, talking to me, through several individuals sparked a flame in me. I birthed Redbaby Publishing, to create and publish my stories and to honor my mother, one of my biggest cheerleaders. *God said now here comes your purpose.* Look what He did. Here's this young girl back in junior high school writing poetry, writing songs, writing stories, who in high school had a teacher who believed in her. This teacher said, "you are a storyteller, there is power in your voice. Consider journalism as a career." Again, in college, and friends and acquaintances all speaking to me on God's behalf. There I was, still half-listening, not ready.

Despite my obstacle course, I graduated from college at 49 with an undergraduate degree in Communication Studies (Journalism). At 52, I graduated again, conferring a graduate degree in Early Childhood Studies. Look at what God designed when I finally listened to him at 57 years old. Forty years after

Reinvented by His Design

the seed was first planted. I'm an author, publisher, advocate, motivational speaker, host of my podcast. Thank you to my mom, Annie Hines, my stepmother Elaine Jones, my bonus grandmother Dorothy Jones, my maternal grandmother Jessie Cade, and my angel and paternal grandmother Martha Curtis. You all taught me to trust my spirit, speak my truth, and walk in my resilience. These women taught me the power of prayer.

Despite me veering off course, God brought me full circle back to the gifts and purpose He charged me with. I am doing the work HE tasked me to do. He reminded me of the promise I made. Thank you to my Lord and Savior for always giving me a seat at the table.

Lisa Jones Harwell

CEO, Redbaby Publishing, Inc.

Host of Journeys with Jones Harwell

https://jonesharwell.com

https://anchor.fm/lisa-harwell

Eve Gomez

Entrepreneur | Radio Talk-Show Host

"Perseverance: The Key to Resilience and Leading Through Challenging Times."

With a passion for business and community, Eve Gomez is a successful business leader, media personality, motivational speaker. She is the owner of EG Spanish Interpreting, LLC which provides Spanish translations and interpretation services in company policy training, courtroom hearings, trials, lawsuits,

"Perseverance: The Key to Resilience and Leading Through Challenging Times."

and medical field. Eve also consults agencies and companies on ways to reach the Latino market, offering over 35 years in Customer Service experience. Eve is also building an E-Commerce business and taking ownership of other types of businesses such as a Credit restoration referral agent and an insurance agent.

Throughout her life, she's had a passion for helping people. She is a community advocate, especially for the elderly, the non-English-speaking people and youth. Eve is very energetic, positive and powerful in the community. As a community leader/activist/mentor and radio host on WLTH radio, and now on her own podcast in several platforms, called "Moments of Inspiration and Motivation with E.V.E.," it enables her to reach out in the broader community and help to improve the quality of life and education. Eve's passion is just that, to help those in need.

Through her profession, she can reach out throughout the state of Indiana and Illinois and now around the country. Her purpose is to educate, inform, motivate, inspire, and help empower others.

To learn more about Eve, you can find her on Google, Facebook, Twitter, Snapchat, Instagram, and LinkedIn. Eve Gomez also has a YouTube channel and podcast, "Moments of Inspiration and Motivation with E.V.E."

For speaking engagements or in need of her other services, contact her via email at evegomezenterprise@gmail.com

"Perseverance: The Key to Resilience and Leading Through Challenging Times."

Coming to America was one of the greatest experiences I ever had. I learned so much in my first year of being in Gary, Indiana, such as the language, currency, and culture. I am also proud to say that I was among the first generation in my family to attend college. As a little girl, I advanced to the first grade after proving to my teacher that I was a fast learner in less than 4 months of residing in the United States. I considered myself to be one bright cookie. Being in school was not always easy, though, as I experienced racism. Many of my peers thought I was White, but others called me derogatory names. They also bullied me as a child, but my love for humanity won the bullies over.

Throughout my childhood, I can say that I spent little time with my parents because my father worked all three shifts in the U.S. Steel Mill and my mother was busy cooking, cleaning, and sewing clothes for my siblings and I. I was left with five brothers at a very young age after my two sisters married. Instead of having five brothers to defend me, I had to learn to defend myself. Thinking about it now makes me laugh because I realize I was always a feisty girl.

I received a public education through middle school and attended a private school in my high school years. My father thought that by me being the only daughter left in the family, I should go to a private school. Our family friends influenced my parents' decision to enroll me in Andrean High School. That was my first encounter with a remarkably diverse school environment. During my sophomore year, my father was laid off from work, so I had to make the tough decision to either go back to public school or pay my way through high school. I worked to take care of my education. I became very sociable and popular among my peers

"Perseverance: The Key to Resilience and Leading Through Challenging Times."

during my time at Andrean. After graduating, I studied business management at Robert Morris Business College, now known as Robert Morris University. My work ethic from such a young age made me choose that major. I learned to work hard from my father, while my mother taught me moral values and unconditional love.

At 26, I married and later had two beautiful children, a boy and a girl. Unfortunately, my marriage did not last long. I divorced 10 years later from my verbally abusive husband because I felt it would be better to raise my children without that type of influence and environment. My family was ashamed of me because I was the first one to divorce in the family. I had to prove to my mother that it was okay to do so and referenced a biblical scripture. Living in an abusive relationship was not healthy for me or my children. I lost everything and move back home, which was a struggle at first. I knew God was on my side and that my strength came from God.

Years later, I experienced two more unhealthy relationships, but always felt that there was something different about me. I learned to endure and persevere through whatever challenges came my way. Another challenge in my life was taking care of my mother and father as they became sick while raising my two children. I realized it was God who allowed me to experience all that I did and later felt that they specifically chose me to be there for my parents. I have been a very spiritual woman since my early adult life, even with not knowing how to grow spiritually. I felt moved to become an elder at my church in 2015, devoting my life to Christ. Throughout the years, I have pushed through and maintained peace within myself while offering it to others. I learned to forgive quickly and love unconditionally by the grace of God. As they say, if they hand you lemons, make lemonade.

"Perseverance: The Key to Resilience and Leading Through Challenging Times"

My interpretation of this simple phrase is to dance in your storm as I have.

When my life demanded that I adjust my lifestyle to meet the needs of my loved ones, I could do so. Out of the necessity for flexibility of time, I quit my 9-5 job and EG Spanish Interpreting, LLC was born. With this business, I could help my parents and many non-English-speaking people in the region. It is customary in the Latino/Hispanic community that one child in a family becomes the interpreter for the parents and possibly older siblings who have not grasped the English language. That is exactly what happened to me. Once I started caring for my parents and realized that their health was declining, my time became priceless and I needed to be available to them. I did not dwell on how I was going to support my family and care for my parents at the same time; I just did it. I have to admit; it was a breath of fresh air not having to report to someone and be under others' rules and regulations. Adjusting to this lifestyle was a financial sacrifice, but it was all worth it.

In November 2018, I lost my home of 12 years and months later my vehicle had given its last breath. Being self-employed has its pros and cons, but I did not sweat the small stuff. I heard God's voice saying to let go of everything and to trust him, so I did. I only kept what was most important to my children and me. After losing my home, I moved in with one of my brothers. I knew God had a greater plan for me, and in the summer of 2019, I got a new car.

Things were stable for a while until the COVID-19 pandemic hit. My interpreting business came to a complete halt, so I was not receiving any income. What was I to do now? I certainly did not

"Perseverance: The Key to Resilience and Leading Through Challenging Times"

sit still and do nothing. I did not stress, instead; I trusted the process. I became a credit

restoration referral agent to teach financial literacy. I also became an insurance agent, offering living benefits. I have been able to help people become financially free through both businesses and have educated and empowered people through my new knowledge.

Thankfully, this was all done virtually, so they could still use me for the greater good without having to travel and be at risk to people. I remained steadfast, prayerful, focused, positive, and joyful, and God answered my prayers with a new home this past summer. I walk by faith and not by sight (2 Corinthians 5:7) because anything is possible (Mathew 19:26).

For the past 3 decades, I remained active in the community, serving on several executive school boards and leading in my church and other non-for-profit organizations. I have blessed many families through my interpreting services, advocacy, mentoring, and empowerment skills. It gives me great peace and satisfaction knowing that I can live my purpose. I am grateful to God for the strength, wisdom, courage, and knowledge he has given me to make a difference in others' lives. I never made things about myself, even in my struggles. I come to tell you I have persevered and endured. The saying, "what doesn't kill you makes you stronger" is what I believe in whole heartedly.

Perseverance unlocked my resilience and has allowed me to take the reins through challenging times. As they say, where there is a will, there is a way, and I know God is a way-maker. I have many more testimonies to share, so stay tuned for my autobiography coming this spring.

"Perseverance: The Key to Resilience and Leading Through Challenging Times"

I leave you with this thought. There are 3 types of people: (1) the one who waits for things to happen, (2) the one who makes things happen, and (3) the one who wonders what happened. Which one are you?

I hope that sharing my story has helped you feel good about yourself and for you to know that you are not alone. Through all the troubles, one can only become stronger!

Dr. Paul W. Dyer

Award-Winning Educator | Community Activist

The Neuro-Black Out

Dr. Paul W Dyer has been teaching and training individuals in human performance on Mental, Emotional, Physical advancement. Dr. Dyer has worked with top tier business professionals to Olympic athletes increase their potentials.

The Neuro-Black Out

Dr. Dyer helps professional people understand the science in the energy of life. Dr. Paul W Dyer has chaired many committees to help communities, individuals rise above different situations and circumstances, from homelessness, prison reform, and domestic violence.

Dr. Paul W Dyer has devoted 40 years to learning and Studying Human Development. Dr. Dyer holds three Ph.D.'s and three master's degrees, and master's certifications in Neuroscience, Neuroanatomy, Stress Management, Psychology, Applied Psychology, Neuro-Linguistics Programming. Grandmaster of Martial Arts, Dr. Paul W Dyer is a Hall of fame Inductee in several national and international martial arts halls of fame. Along with many accomplishments are these:

The Neuro-Black Out

- **Professor at World Union of Scientific Associations**
- **International Peace Committee for Law, Justice and Human Rights (Ambassador)**
- **World Traditional Medical Association (Doctor)**
- **Doctor with Canadian Health and Sciences**
- **United Nations Peace Ambassador**
- **United States Director for Global Peace University**
- **International Association of Top Professionals**
- **Awarded Dr Paul W Dyer Top Strategist of 2020**
- **Scientific research Adviser for Presidential, Governor, legislative political races.**

Dr Paul W Dyer has written several self-help books and is a consistent contributor to a good deal of news and online health magazines. Through the education of others, we can set a fire in motion to change the world.

Dr. Paul W Dyer is The United States Executive Director for The Federal Association of the Advancement of Visible Minorities. Dr. Paul W Dyer above all is a father of 9 children, a grandfather, a husband, a friend and military veteran. Dr. Paul has dedicated his life to protecting and opening the gateway that all can walk through by practicing and training.

Dr Paul W Dyer is the CEO of Whole Life Training and Host of Bridges Live Podcast Live Show.

Bridges Live Produces Several shows on:

- IHeart,
- Apple Podcast
- YouTube

The Neuro-Black Out

The shows are:

- Mental Health Mondays
- Free@Last
- You Be The Judge
- Voices To Be Heard

Black Coffee Conversations

My Goal: To build a world that understands oneself and stomps out trauma. To develop policies for black America to move forward.

The Neuro-Black Out

To be a human being is tough in an opposing obstructive environment. To have trauma, your outcome to elevation to your next level is tougher. Now close your eyes and be black in America today, your chemicals in your body are on a whole different level. I promise you this until you understand and start releasing your trauma, the success you seek in anything will fail. This is not a scare tactic to get you to adhere, but a scientific fact on how the mind, spirit, body works. The training and practice you can develop will raise the frequency to live successfully. I am sure you have read that if you don't recognize the surrounding darkness, it will cover your light. The light that is talked about or is being talked about is the cellular connection your body creates when it's in tune (balance) and the white light shines when you close your eyes in prayer or mediation.

I believe in rainbows and dolphins and sunny days to come trust me, but what is often scary to me when beings don't think their body, mind, spirit has an emotional voice and quiet. It by so call blind logic. These things are emotional death, caused by trauma not being recognized. I understand how fearful it can be to allow yourself to be free to admit you have not dealt with the trauma of being human or being black in America because many are afraid of getting hurt. Stop living in your fears and allow yourself to be successful in life. In my education, I have learned that positive and negative emotions are associated with internal organs. One key to good health is to notice the emotional energies that live in the organs and to transform the negative emotional energies into positive virtues. It is believing that we are all born with the virtues of love, gentleness, kindness, respect, honesty, fairness, justice, and righteousness. There is a renewed collective calling to achieve a level and strength of personal transformation that ultimately impacts the global reality, transformation that provides both deliverance from personal suffering and a clear understanding of how changes at the fulcrum point of individual

The Neuro-Black Out

awareness will impact the morpho-genetic field. As units of Human bio-circuitry, we are the culmination of a variety of life-force energy systems. The new frontier of healing lies knowing that these systems are not fully connected. The Human heart-body-mind integrates the energetic nature of consciousness that fosters all life via bio-circuitry. The circuitry is the delivery system that integrates this Source Intelligence, translating this energetic electromagnetic life-force into the bio-informational matrix that is the vibratory infrastructure of the Human hologram.

The thing I speak of is the science that was hidden from you in plain sight for centuries. Even if you started practicing so-called yoga or eating veggies or even deep into your practice religion, the reason you are failing in your efforts is that your body is still holding onto the trauma like old birthday cards given by your grandma.

I have studied and practice the laws of the universe and it has opened the gateway of joy to success. I can teach you the geometry and physics of the living sciences to open that window to virtually see into the creator's gifts that are waiting for you. Others think and talk about barriers and constrictions, I think it's human constructs that are creating lines of divisions on a physical plan and molecular. We now know that protons travel over thermodynamic barriers. We also know that temperature was a factor. To me, protons have active partners that they communicate with now and over the history of time. These particles are connected in consciousness form, which creates a vector. They connect particles over vast distances. When actions are performed on the particle, corresponding changes are observed in the other simultaneously. This would allow for rapid processes like the fast exchange of information between the two. Particles or better known as electrons and photons, exist as

The Neuro-Black Out

waves but can also behave like particles. In a manner of speaking, they are both waves and particles. When in waveform it is also vibrations. Therefore, consciousness is developed around the brain and the brain hemispheres pick up the wave signal and can transmit and decode it. This is transmitted in the body from our crown down the spine. The only way we can obstruct these actions from occurring is by rendering them block by our own divisions we construct from our physical, emotional self (the Trauma not recognized). Chemical and molecularity these actions are waiting for you to open yourself up to God, the maker of the universe (Your Success). Our own imprisonments have severed these connections. When I am in my meditated state, I am open to all the signals of creation. These waves come into space, call dark matter, and fill the space with energy. This action then contributes to our genetic codes that are constantly evolving. When the organ keeps releasing the information triggered by a chemical reaction, it dispatches the feelings of the lower vibration understanding in the residence of our collaboration of our external cells being blocked by the phase conjugation. These processes involved the acquisition of experience directly connected to our organ vibration.

These reflections are not governed by theory, but the laws of the universe govern them.

Scars remind us about where we have been, not where we are going. The problem is that the trauma that is not understood is reflected in our biochemistry governed by the universal law. Through the constraints of the physical reality, the vibration frequencies have become separated from the neutral state, creating the state of duality or polarity. Since there are only two polarities of energy, accordingly there are only two emotions, Love and Fear. That which is not Love is Fear. Spirit, in a totally unified state, contains both positive and negative energy. These

The Neuro-Black Out

energies reflect one another within the wholeness of the Source, which is the state of oneness. Separation comes about through resistance, which results in the division of energy into polarities. This culminates in the experience of duality. Each part you don't like has a gift to give you and is appropriate in certain situations. When we embrace a quality within ourselves, then people with the same quality can no longer plug into us. This frees them to experience you, and you are free to experience them. To truly love yourself, you must get your negative emotions out. If we own hate and evil in ourselves, we wouldn't need to project it onto another person. Compassion heals and reveals our true essence to evolve Spirit in Action!

Life is hard and corrupted. What is hard is our outlook on the sickness of the things that have polluted our mind, body, and spirits. Pleasure, fear clouds us, and worry. Only the bliss is causeless, which you can be if you did not care for yourself or anyone in life. Well, settling for pain and pleasure, the bliss of cluelessness founds the fear and worry only could have. It is because you have not found or not realized yourself. What is realization? Realization means perpetual natural, effortless self-knowledge. I will explain what effortless knowledge is. It is all that is felt without memory of anything ever before. Natural knowledge is universal acceptance. Realizations are permanent. The realization of consciousness means the end of faith and duality. Listen to these words carefully, for these are like sowing seeds. You will see its fruits in due course. All existence expresses the consciousness of the one who is the knower of consciousness, the occupier and the occupied are not two, but one. That one from where this space originates is within us. The mind has no birth or death. Mind means language. It stops when the flow of language starts. The same applies to the word. The word originates from space in the mind, from Consciousness. Your behavior is the prey to confusion and rationalization of fear

The Neuro-Black Out

and worry, but most of all your ideas. Consciousness is not an idea it is an awareness of the truth that is connected to all things as above as below.

When we reflect on life in this human form, take moments to not see, hear, or even think, but feel our internal truth. It is just like this; it's being able to sit peacefully and get up peacefully and be content with what you have; it's that which makes our life as a daily experience something that is joyful and not suffering. And this is how we can live in the realization of consciousness and faith; beliefs are not needed.

Because of the genetic modification of our DNA, the Human bio-computer cannot sustain its molecular structure in a state of super-consciousness. The reconnection of circuitry restores the fundamental energy supply intrinsic to the Human ability to achieve and sustain conscious evolution into the new paradigm. This electromagnetic energy is integrated into the body through meridians or circuits, to be translated by the energy centers into bio-informational signals for the endocrine system to utilize.

The circuitry does not begin and end around the Human energy field. Each circuit is spherical and intersects with another spherical field of conscious energy, which interacts with another, as part of an electromagnetic intelligence system that encompasses all - from the subatomic to the multi-universal, the wheels within wheels. Each sphere of consciousness is a hologram fractal of Source Intelligence.

I know I have said a lot in this chapter, much might understand, and a good deal of might just get lost. No matter the place it is ok. I have driven away all of this information from, taken away from you, and blinded from you. Therefore, this chapter called "The Neuro Black Out." I am here to help you understand your greatness. There is a science to life. Our life is all about self-discovery within society. Discover the ultimate being you really are.

You can reach Dr. Paul W. Dyer at 301-789-3174 or email at Drpaulwdyer@gmail.com.

Cortne' Lee Smith

Award Winning-Entrepreneur |Relationship Strategist

Beyond Loss

It was eighty-nine days later, and I still avoided the reality of my husband's death. I initially worked 16-20-hour days to ensure I was too exhausted to think of anything that would interrupt my sleep. I used work as a shield to get out of conversations or outings with Friends or Family. This day was going just like every other day since April 4th, 2012 I initially

Beyond Loss

overbooked the calendar that would allow me to miss my ride to New Orleans for a holiday extended weekend. However, by noon all my clients had called to reschedule for after the holidays. My ride called moments later to inform me I could get on the Amtrak and get picked up in New Orleans. At that moment I didn't give thought to yesterday or tomorrow, but gave a "YES", grabbed one of the many overnight bags I kept packed for work, jumped into a cab, and was pulling off the train platform 45 minutes later.

Did you know that a regular six-hour drive is almost twelve hours on the train? My normal routine of busy was broken. All I had time to do was think. First thought was how was I going to get myself back on the next train back to Atlanta. Eventually, I took advantage of this time to clean out and respond to voicemails plus emails that had my storage full. Catch up on some Netflix shows that allowed my mind to wander. The entire weekend from winning at the casino tables with enough money to cover more than what I would have spent on the weekend trip, dancing and singing through the shows, to sitting capturing a picture in THE Voice chair that was a part of the expo. I didn't just survive the holiday break; it opened me up to thrive again.

Now fast forward to November 16th. Here I sat with my coworker and now brother in love. The conversation went a little something like this. "I notice you are happy and moving forward after the passing of your husband." Then it was said, "My brother is having a hard time coping with the passing of his wife and I do not know what to say to him to help him." He requested me to

Beyond Loss

talk with his brother under the pretense of getting my truck repaired. FYI: because his brother, my now husband, is a mobile mechanic. I agreed to the charade, and a date would have said repairs done. Ten days later the table was prepared and my broken down 1994 2500 Silverado Chevrolet was ready to be worked on running to its full potential. On the counter in the kitchen, I had three crock pots going to feed the natural man. Upon his arrival, I was still dressed in my work attire to conduct business. During his diagnosis, we chatted and laughed about my lack of automotive maintenance skills. Jumping in the mechanic's truck to head to the parts store, the lively conversation continued.

In hindsight, I know New Orleans served as my process and my friend served as my iron to heat the word within me to push out the impurities to return to a pure iron state. It was a tangible purging of emails, but most importantly it gave me time to purge thoughts and perceptions of what being a widow was to look like. It freed me to take a gamble and win big, not just faster pockets with some extra green. I left with the ability to still see greener pastures still ahead for me.

If we take a moment and reflect on the charade of meeting my current husband. We can understand iron sharpens iron. However, the scripture Proverb 27:17 is dated back to a specific time when iron had various compositions. Certain iron has to encounter each other to sharpen another. At that specific time, his brother could not serve as his sharpening block. It was my assignment to come in at the right angle to help fine-tune and

Beyond Loss

make him aware of the healing he needed on the grief journey. I served as his guide to look at his now and not become a prisoner of the past and others' beliefs. We walk together each day beyond our loss, sharpen each other's perspective to see better for our tomorrows and cherish our now's.

Take a moment to visualize with me for a moment a 19 pcs kitchen knife set. In most knife sets, six of the knives can perform the same function. However, all the other knives have a specific edge to be used for specific cuts. In this knife set comes a sharpener with rough ridges to run along each knife to keep up the curve and cut of each blade in the set. Where we fall short is attempting to be a knife that functions in all situations. If we can accept that we have specific assignments in life; not limitations, but our lane, which is designed for us to win. When we operate outside the purpose, they designed us for, ultimately, we can cause further damage to the vessels we seek to help and cause damage to ourselves at the same time. His brother recognized it did not equip him to sharpen him.

As a Relationship and Life Coach, I am assigned as a sharpener to restore the edge and point back to the iron that has been through grief and loss. I am equipped with many ridges that scrape off the residue of the past. At times I feel very abrasive as I rub up against your excuses to not make stabs into your future. Other times I get deep down to the handle of your blade to cut away the stains of shame and regret to remove the victim mentality that keep one from chopping life into digestible bites to see victory in all situations and circumstances. I will require you

Beyond Loss

to come out of your safe space in the block of knives to be used according to your purpose.

Cortne' Lee Smith

"Relationship Mechanic"
Grief Strategists | Life & Relationship Coach | Media Host & Executive Producer | Trainer |Speaker
Relationship Service Station, LLC.
Website: relationservicestation.com
Email: cortne@relationshipservicestation.com
Business Phone: 678.718.5019
Social Media Platforms: Facebook, Instagram, YouTube

Dr. Clarice Kavanaugh, Ph.D., MBA
Management Consultant, Executive Business Coach, Trainer

Taking your Great to Greater: Level UP

Clarice Kavanaugh is a native of Chicago, Il and has lived in Long Beach, CA for 37 years. Clarice has spent her career in

Taking your Great to Greater: Level UP

Sales and Marketing primarily in the pharmaceutical industry for over 35 years.

As an experienced influencer, is where Clarice birthed a career change and stepped into her destiny as a change maker. Exiting the Corporate world to a classroom setting, as a university professor, Executive Coach, Trainer, Motivational Speaker and Radio Talk Show host. Clarice learned the ability to change the perspective of her audience through engagement and classroom synergy.

Having in hand over 30 years of experience in sales and marketing, she learned the benefits of human connection. Her magical abilities of connecting staff/students, whether in a corporate or classroom setting, led to improved employee/student engagement outcomes.

Since 1980, her career in sales led to the choice of facilitating classroom offerings with a concentration of Organizational Change and Leadership. Renown organizations often seek after her both private/public sector, as a facilitator of leadership behaviors, team building, and communication workshops with a specialty in Diversity and Inclusion in the Workplace.

Clarice promotes and foster individual and organizational effectiveness by developing and offering an array of innovative and diverse programs to support the organization's employee training and development, partnerships, and organizational enrichment. Ensuring results reaches the next level.

Taking your Great to Greater: Level UP

Her passion is in the development of people and taking them to the next level of their career, as well as organizational success. Combining her business analytics and strategic abilities, she has continued to prove that success is her guiding principle.

Clarice's teaching and coaching modality includes a no nonsense approach and accountability, while emphasizing the benefits of Intellectual Excitement, which invokes clarity of learning materials and Interpersonal Rapport, which increases awareness, engagement and motivation and enjoyment through communication strategies to foster independent learning, acceptance, and willingness to apply material.

The biggest struggle of taking your great to greater is understanding that you do not differ from the people you want to rejuvenate, elevate, or rebuild. The same power you are telling people they have, exist also in yourself. How often have you sat down with a person you managed regardless of the setting and encouraged them and help them see the great in themselves. Every time you do, you are taking your great to greater. It is impossible and unrealistic to sharpen iron without sharpening yours in the process.

You may think that sounds simple, and you are right it is. The key is not to come pray to three things, distractions, unfocused and loss of self. Loss of self is the easiest of the three, which is why you are distracted and lose focus.

Taking your Great to Greater: Level UP

Taking your great to greater and leveling up is the appreciation you have of yourself at tall times. When I have a client that I am coaching or mentoring, I do my best to dive deep into the emotional part. They are sitting in front of me, on zoom, with a wish of list of what they are trying to do, with no actual idea of how to get there. They struggle with taking their great to great and leveling up. Therefore, they hire me- they do not know it, but they soon find out, no matter how great they think they are, no matter how big their titles are, or they want them to be, they still have a strong desire to go to greater and Level Up. I have never met a person who did not have a next level.

The more you give, the greater you will get. I will say that again, Giver = Greater, No deposit, no return. You may think, well I can get without giving and still be great, I can give you examples of how that will soon backfire, but I am only here to focus on the magnificent in you.

Ok, I will give you one example. Your ATM card, no matter how much money you THINK you have in the bank, your great enters an amount to withdraw, and the screen reads insufficient fund, even though you seem confused, because you just knew you had the money. The ATM operates on that simple system, no deposit, no return. The ATM is Greater. As you stand there scanning your brain, training to log on to your online banking, you think when the last time you made a deposit and how much were you taking out and not giving back to Mr. ATM. You have reached a moment of truth and an Aha moment in time.

Taking your Great to Greater: Level UP

Now that we are on the same page, that is how your Great to Greater works. You must keep giving to be greater. The more you help, support, random acts of kindness, mentor, coach, give an employee a kind of work of encouragement, the little things all add up and will take you to your GREATER.

If you do not appreciate yourself, you will not, cannot ever go to Greater and will soon lose your Great. It is all an inside job. It is not a mystery it is magical Every time I work with a new client or do a presentation in front of the room my Great become Greater- I feel the power of Leveling up. That power is something that God has given me. He made me see my great, and he has empowered me to give it to others and that takes me to my greater and the ability to level up. It is no small deed to convince influential people to collaborate with you and allow you to help them take them to their great. In doing so, you know you are taking your Greater and sharing it, whether you are invoicing someone or doing pro bono. It does not lessen your reward of greatness. If you talk to the Greater folk in life, ask them how many things they did freely before they got to where they are now. That makes them great. There is not a story that can be found that your hero or shero was a person who gave of themselves to others not expecting anything in return. That is the longevity, that how you can stay viable for decades and not days.

As you manage, coach, motivate, and encourage people, you see God is in control and has given you a toolbox of skills and talent. Do not be afraid to use it. Taking your great to greater involves risk taking, thinking outside the box, strategic analysis, and transparency. These are the tools you prayed for, they are a

Taking your Great to Greater: Level UP

gift from God and not be taken lightly of for grant it. How many people wish they were you or had the talents you have? Think about it. Many times, people are given gifts and they become afraid of these gifts that were given unconditionally and misuse them or under use them. That is what I meant by backfire, when you lose yourself. God's assignment is for you is to take your great to greater. Do not be afraid to level up.

    I am speaking from experience; I was afraid to level up. I was afraid of taking my great to greater. I was great at taking others to the next level, but I did not realize that each time I did, I went to another level also, but I did not believe it. I had to do my best to see myself as others see me and realize that it was okay to be to acknowledge the good too great to greater things that I was accomplishing. I have been told over and over what I could not do as a single parent; I did not believe them, outwardly, but inside I struggled. Through my struggle I continued to move forward and not stay stagnate and fight to find and embrace my great. It was my aha moment., after all did not, I tell people this all the time. I was the ultimate cheerleader, coach, strategist, now to do these things for myself. I had to coach myself through a doctoral program after I retired. I had plenty of naysayers and now I am a university professor. I took my great to the greater.

 One thing I highly recommend to my clients is to stay away from negative people. The negativity of what I could not do has distracted me. I am sure you have had people encouraging you to fail. The ones telling saying you are a rock star you do not hear; it is the ones saying you are not. Do not justify your plan to great or your elevation to greater. Never explain yourself to people that

Taking your Great to Greater: Level UP

are not greater than you. They cannot help you; you cannot grow and you cannot help others. You will be stuck in the self-doubt quicksand of life. Remember your assignment, take your great to greater, level up. You prayed for greatness and every time you give, you will get greater. I tell my clients this all the time. They fight me and say I do not understand, and I say, just try helping people and engage. People will see the difference before you will sometimes. This is your Aha moment. Cherish it, own it, thank God for it. The magic appears, and the greater is forming. You prayed for this moment; the power is within you. Go out and make it happen. It' never too late, you are never too old and never give up. Your great will be greater and you smiled when you thought great was good enough. Congratulations you Leveled Up!

Please contact the author for speaking, consulting or coaching services.

clarice@thekavanaughgroup.com

www.thekavanaughgroup.com

Toya Jordan

Entrepreneur | Financial Expert

Building Generational Wealth Starts in The Mind

Toya is a native of New Orleans, Louisiana, where she still lives. She works with Primerica Financial Services as a Regional Vice President and Registered Securities Principal. Toya is a visionary, mentor, and lead trainer of team "Just Do It" within the organization. Toya is the Regional Vice President of

Building Generational Wealth Starts in The Mind

Community Partnership with the Signature Entrepreneurs & Mastermind Group. She promotes the temper to change the mindset and outcome of how individuals build assets and achieve financial prosperity within the group. During her leisure time, Toya works with the local community by creating workshops on monetary education, closing the wealth gap, and coaching individuals on how to become entrepreneurs within the financial service industry. She also donates her time by teaching financial literacy to high school students through a workshop she created called "How Money Works". It teaches adolescents about assets versus liabilities, avoiding the credit trap, and how to create financial wealth during their lifetime. Despite all her accomplishments, Toya would tell anyone her greatest attribute is being a mother to her beautiful daughter, Taya Amani. Toya strongly believes her purpose is to help individuals, especially those in communities of color, build a legacy of generational wealth, and she is passionate about consulting with people in obtaining financial independence.

On a 'Super Sunday' my tank was empty, and I had no choice but to stop for gas at a crowded filling station. The cashier line stretched long because of my fellow New Orleanians looking to cash-in on a Powerball award of $560,000,000. I simply wanted coffee and needed gas and so there I was standing in a line that felt as if it was a half-mile long. In New Orleans, 'Super Sunday' is a big deal. On this particular Sunday, everyone was 'fresh to death,' as we would say in the 7th Ward. The Indians were the chief attraction. You see, in New Orleans, we celebrate Native Americans through dance and elaborate

Building Generational Wealth Starts in The Mind

costumes as a way to pay homage to Native Americans for providing our ancestors with refuge from slavery.

Because the line was unbearably long and I needed to occupy my mind, I gave close consideration to the lottery patrons' fashion. (I must note that the owners of the gas station or even the cashier were not native New Orleanians). I noticed customers were wearing Gucci, Prada, Chanel, Jordan's, and Louis Vuitton. They dressed even the infants head to toe in Ralph Lauren. I pondered internally, how many of us have ownership of the things we buy? While standing in line, people were feeling hopeful about becoming instant millionaires. While eavesdropping on the woman's discussion in line before me, she talked about how much she hated her job as a teacher because her compensation was nearly nothing. If by chance she won the lottery, she would purchase a Bentley and retire her mother, 76 years of age. When it was her turn in line, she told the clerk how she prayed in church for God to bless her with the winning numbers, and she was spending her last $150 on purchasing her tickets.

As I paid for my gas and coffee, I walked out to a crowded parking lot and witnessed the cleanest cars in the neighborhood. Cadillac with Vogue tires, the most beautiful pearl white Porsche, but my favorite was the candy-apple red 1977 Cutlass on 22-inch Asanti rims. While pumping my gas, a homeless guy asked everyone for loose change or a dollar to spare. You could

Building Generational Wealth Starts in The Mind

barely hear him because of the loud base blasting from several expensive sound systems. The scene was buzzing, and so was my mind.

I got in my car and drove down the city blocks of the 7th Ward, ruminating on my people's mindset regarding financial literacy:

- Do we genuinely comprehend the contrast between assets, liabilities, and net worth? To have stock in anything means we have ownership.

- Are we owners or perpetual consumers? Systematic inequalities created the wealth gap in the African American community; however, through financial literacy and economic empowerment, we can change the narrative and outcome.

- Do we know where to put our money and make it work for us? They did not create financial institutions to teach us financial literacy; their responsibility is to sell products.

- Are we willing to educate ourselves? Education on using dollars to develop assets such as mutual funds, stocks, bonds, real estate, business ownership, life insurance, annuities, retirement, and education accounts has to be part of our financial literacy beliefs.

Methodically, we were taught to have a checking and savings account at our local bank or credit union, take part in our employer-sponsored retirement plan, purchase a single-family home, and save a few dollars under our mattresses for a rainy day. Because of this lack of knowledge, we tend to invest conservatively in certificates of deposits or leave thousands of

Building Generational Wealth Starts in The Mind

dollars in our checking accounts. Yet, the fundamental Rule of 72 and compound interest teaches us it will take a few lifetimes before it ever created any wealth in those types of investments. The outcome of that type of thinking crushes net worth and the psyches in our communities.

Having a considerable number of dollars to become rich or receive a miracle from God by winning the lottery is not financial logic. Yet, many adopt a 'fake it till you make it' mindset - which is also illogical. This thinking suggests that if we dress in designer clothes, shoes, purses, have an extravagant vehicle, hair, nails, and lashes that in some way or another we closely resemble, we are in turn [hood] rich.

Even when individuals earn a good salary, there are still concerns about financial literacy. It is seductive to be dazzled by our salaries. However, often after investigating the overall picture, it usually shows thousands of dollars in student loan debt, house notes, car notes, children's school tuition, insurance, and did I neglect to specify taxes. We all are aware of athletes, artists, or individuals in corporate jobs making thousands or millions of dollars that had to file bankruptcy or sell off all their assets to avoid prosecution.

We must learn the skill of getting our dollars to work for us. When we achieve this aim, we need to teach it to our children. Schooling should require proficiency in financial literacy. Understanding ways of managing money, how to financially

Building Generational Wealth Starts in The Mind

plan/budget, knowing your credit, having a course of action to get out of debt, and building a low-maintenance business separate from your corporate occupation are non-negotiable requisites.

The foundation of our financial game plan must comprise the following:

- Term life insurance that's eight to ten times your current annual income
- An emergency account of three to six months of income
- Retirement plan and having a Roth or Traditional IRA
- Education accounts for your kids
- Homeownership (an asset)
- Understanding rental property versus a single-family home
- Budgeting that prioritizes savings over spending

My aim as a Regional Vice President and Registered Securities Principal is to change the 'wishing to get rich' mindset where the lottery, dressing in the finest clothing, or driving the most extravagant vehicle supersedes sound financial planning. I consistently teach our community how we can own the corner stores, have stock in those companies we use, hold the properties and businesses that line our city streets, have a retirement plan that will keep up with inflation, a life insurance policy that would create an estate, and give our children a head starts by having an advance degree with no financial obligation. Financial literacy

Building Generational Wealth Starts in The Mind

equals economic empowerment, which changes our community. We must be intentional.

Author contact info:

Email: **Queensrule365@yahoo.com**

Senita V. Carter

Finding My IT!

Senita V. Carter is a Licensed Insurance Agent / Final Expense Specialist. She is a graduate of Benedict College—Columbia, SC, where she received a Bachelor of Arts Degree in English and Webster University–St. Louis, Mo, where she received a Master

Finding My IT!

of Arts Degree in Community Counseling. She is also a Notary Public for the state of South Carolina.

On a more personal note… Senita is divorced and the mother of two ridiculously handsome young men, who she loves being a "Boy Mom" to. She is always willing to lend a helping hand to anyone in need. Which is why she goes out every day to educate individuals on the importance of insurance and legacy building. She always looks for opportunities to make a difference in other people's lives. When she's not helping others, she enjoys sports of all kinds with her son's, spending time with family, watching documentaries, traveling, and getting pampered every chance she can. Senita is a child of God and looks to him to help navigate her life. She believes we all have special gifts and talents and there is a purpose for all of our lives. It is up to us to exercise our gifts and talents and walk in our purpose; whatever it maybe.

I remember like it was yesterday…growing up and living with my grandparents was a sheer joy which left me with invaluable lesson's and all kinds of fond memories. But it did not lose how that came to be on me either. My mother and father were on their way to being divorced when my siblings, mother and I moved in with my grandparents. I couldn't have been only 4 or 5 years old. There was a lot of transition and unanswered questions during that time. Of course, growing up during those times, you could not ask questions; let alone get an explanation for anything because you valued your life. It wasn't until later on in life when my parents felt I could understand the situation when they; separately sat me down and gave their versions of their story.

Finding My IT!

There was a lot that transpired during my formative years while living with my grandparent's. You see… I am the first grandchild on my mother's side and the eldest of my siblings. So, with my birth order also came a lot of responsibility; none of which I asked for at that time, because I wanted to be a kid too, but nonetheless it did. Some of those responsibilities involved cooking for a tribe of people, cleaning the house, caring for my siblings and doing laundry. Oh! I forgot to tell ya'll my aunts and uncles were living in the house at the time as well. However; I am very grateful for those experiences, because they are the foundation that I continue to build my life upon today.

Every Friday, like clockwork, my mother and grandmother would get together and pool their money together to pay the household bills. This was my first exposure to fiscal responsibility. While watching them do this, they would both say to me "child you are living your best life and you don't know it." Of course, I didn't understand nor could I fathom what they were talking about, because all I knew at the time was, I wasn't wearing name brand / designer clothes, couldn't take part in many extra-curricular activities in school or any other childhood whelms that I wanted to indulge in.

Now that I'm an adult with my own children; I can clearly see what they were talking about. It's because of them I am leaning on their principles. I haven't always gotten it right, but because of them I have something to draw upon. In the Biblical text which grounds the basis of this anthology–"Iron Sharpens Iron"-it states, "As iron sharpens iron, so one person sharpens another"- Proverbs 27:17 (NIV). In the early

Finding My IT!

recollections of my growing up, I didn't know that my Purpose would somehow be tied to my mother and my grandmother's fiscal fitness. Another memory that comes to mind, and this one is key, because this is where "Finding My IT" was birth. This took some time to realize, but IT came full circle.

Just like the monthly bills were paid every month, so was my grandmother's insurance policy. I remember this white man named Mr. Brown used to come to the house every month to collect money from my grandmother. Mr. Brown was my grandmother's Insurance Agent (Debit Agent) to be exact. He was very nice and didn't seem to have a problem with being around us when he came. I guess you are nice when money's involved. This practice of collecting payments was very common; especially in the African American community, and is still practiced today.

With my mother and my grandmother being the original iron sharpeners in my formative years, I had somewhere to start my journey of discovering my own Iron. After many years of serving in an administrative / customer service capacity, I always helped others, because that's what I've always done. While helping others always gave me a sense of satisfaction and pleasure, I somehow still felt unfulfilled. There was always that feeling of knowing there was more that was required of me, but I couldn't put my finger on what it was. There were several instances where a career in insurance was presented to me; but

Finding My IT!

the timing wasn't right, or I'd brush the idea off all together. Meanwhile, during this period, God placed people of significance in my life and each time, it left me with something that would sharpen my iron just a bit more.

While things were changing in my job, so was my countenance. After years of being in an environment where I was doing what I needed to do to provide for me and my children, timing and the right opportunity collided. It was then that I took a leap of faith and went to work for myself in the field of insurance. I can honestly say the decision to leap was one of the best decisions of my life. There's nothing more empowering than taking control of your life and shaping your destiny. I didn't realize how my move would affect my family. To my surprise, everyone was thrilled for me and equally proud, because of the courage it took for me to trust something / someone bigger than me. I come from a family where everyone play's it safe, so making a move like this was definitely against the norm and was an enormous deal. It's because of my influencer's and experiences over the years that it prepared me for such a time as this.

In my case and so many other cases, identifying "iron-like" traits in oneself can be very difficult, because of the way we view ourselves and the value we place on how we are viewed by others. If you live in an environment that is void of anything positive, then identifying iron-like traits will be almost impossible. Most often we are "products of our environment" good or bad, but nonetheless; there's an Iron in you. A positive self-image, confidence in oneself and belief in a higher power

Finding My IT!

will serve you well on your discovery to finding what will fulfill you and set you on your path to your purpose. Mostly when we're looking for something or that "IT" we overlook the obvious within ourselves only for it to be identified by others. It takes an Iron to recognize the Iron in you.

When I go to service my clients, I go with the willingness to help in any way that I can by being professional, using my active listening skills, displaying empathy, and showing a knowledge of my products and services. The aim is to always provide them with outstanding customer service, secure their insurance needs, and close the deal. Sometimes it extends beyond that; such as helping a client secure medical attention, taking them to the bank, run errands, or just be a listening ear. To some this may sound like the job of Social Worker instead of an Insurance Agent. I can assure it's not! It's just some of the things that I've been able to assist with while doing my job as an Insurance Agent. It's called making an Impact!

As a Licensed Insurance Agent / Final Expense Specialist, I assist individuals with Life Insurance. Currently, I'm licensed in South Carolina, North Carolina, Georgia, Maryland, and Tennessee, with the ability to work Nationwide. I offer Whole Life and Term Insurance to people ages 0-85 with Great, Good, Marginal or even Terminal Health Conditions. All Health Conditions Approved. No Medical Exams Required. Guaranteed Approval. I also offer a plan with a concierge service attached to help families save 30% - 80% on all Final Expense costs and Living Benefits as well. Insurance is where legacies are created.

Finding My IT!

Sometimes we fall short because of getting a late start in planning, however we can have something in place to be put away nicely and buried with dignity instead of relying on our families or using "GoFundMe" as a burial plan. Let's leave a LEGACY instead of BILL'S behind. I offer a No Excuse Plan.

If you desire information on any of our products and services or would like to use your "iron-like traits" and your God-given gifts and talent to become an Insurance Agent like myself, I encourage you to contact me TODAY!!!!!

Senita V. Carter, MA
Licensed Insurance Agent / Final Expense Specialist
The SVC Group
Email: senitav@yahoo.com
Business Phone: (803) 479-0696
Social Media Platforms: Facebook, LinkedIn, Instagram, Twitter

Bestselling Author Vincent O. Leggett
Admiral at Blacks of the Chesapeake

Black History Sharpens American History

As the Chaplain for the Signature Entrepreneurs and Masterminds, I approached my chapter with a spiritual lens. I've sought to take the wise principle of being sharpened by one another to a different level.

Proverbs 27:17 KJV

Black History Sharpens American History

"Iron sharpeneth iron; so a man sharpeneth the countenance of his friend."

Vincent O. Leggett is the president and CEO of the Leggett Group USA, a consulting firm that specializes in government relations, public affairs, and environmental advocacy. Vince is a regulated lobbyist with the Maryland General Assembly, with focus areas of equity in educational funding; clean energy; and environmental, historic, and cultural preservation.

Vince is also the founder and president of the Blacks of the Chesapeake Foundation. BOCF documents the significant contributions of African Americans in the maritime and seafood industries and educates and inspires the next generation of local activists. The Library of Congress and the U.S. Congress have designated BOCF as a Local Legacy Project, and the Governor of Maryland commissioned Vince an honorary Admiral of the Chesapeake. Through

BOCF, Vince provides training in diversity, equity, and inclusion initiatives, and continues the tradition of storytelling of African-American history and culture.

With a career spanning over 40 years serving the Maryland area, Vince has held positions in K-16 educational administration and executive leadership roles in assisted living and affordable housing. For 10 years, he served as division chief at the Maryland Department of Natural Resources.

Black History Sharpens American History

Vince earned a B.S. in Urban Planning and Community Development from Morgan State University and a Master's in Public Administration from Central Michigan University. He has undertaken additional training through the University of Michigan Multi-Cultural Leadership Development Initiative, along with the Executive Director Development Training through the Center of Government Services at Rutgers University. Vince and his wife, Aldena, make their home in Annapolis, Maryland. He serves as Chaplain for the City of Annapolis Fire Department and as a board member of the Chesapeake Legal Alliance.

Black History Sharpens American History
February 21, 2021

When I consider the meaning of this axiom of wisdom and truth, and measure it against the course of my life, I can't help but see it as more than mutual support among brothers. For me, the call to share in strength has always meant using the pride instilled in me by family to passionately uplift the accurate history of African Americans. We have to be more intentional about correcting the countenance -- or face -- of American history. After all, Black history is American history, and American history is Black history. They cannot be told separately or considered complete without the other.

African Americans know that their history merits the same honor and respect as the "founding fathers" history that they taught us all. We now need school systems, governments, and all our institutions to see the value of this inclusive mindset. My sense of responsibility towards this goal was the driving force behind the Blacks of the Chesapeake Foundation. I founded BOCF in 1984 to advocate for preservation, to inspire the next generation of activists, and to celebrate our cultural history. BOCF is smashing the myth that African Americans and marginalized citizens do not care about the environment.

African Americans and whites alike have been shielded from honest American history. That is why our heritage must be told as collective, parallel stories, for the benefit of all. This narrative is countering the adverse effects of silencing African American history. I am amplifying the many unheard voices of men and women whose lives have been sharpened by the noble Chesapeake Bay.

Black History Sharpens American History

I am a native-born Marylander, with an innate understanding of life over the decades here for my African American community and a wish to preserve its unwritten history. Long before the abolition of slavery, the bay region played a major role in enslaved African Americans' search for freedom and a better life. I have explored historically significant sites on Maryland's Eastern Shore, which include several "stops" of the Underground Railroad. I spent years traveling the deep and shallow reaches of the Chesapeake region, and as a fellow waterman, they welcomed me into thriving and struggling shoreline communities. I've had conversations with hundreds of African American bay workers, business owners, and family leaders. For much of the 20th century, African Americans made up most workers in oyster and crab-processing houses, and their stories were largely passed down orally and through family histories. The more I heard about their way of life, the more I understood how the older generation's wisdom and culture might become lost.

I am not the first descendant of slaves to want to show the true face of African American life in the 1800s and 1900s. It won't be found in the history textbooks of most American classrooms, where the white perspective has had an erasing effect. But it exists in the hearts of those of us who are only a generation or two removed from the plantation. We rely on ourselves to preserve the truths and honor those who lived in that time. In this way, African Americans have always sharpened the countenance of American history. The history and heritage of the African American experience has hidden in plain sight. My life's work has been to seek the truths that shine light on the cracks and crevices in American history.

That was exactly my intention when I wrote my book *The Chesapeake Bay Through Ebony Eyes* 20 years ago. One man

Black History Sharpens American History

who whose words, history, and heart inspired my book is the old waterman, Captain Earl White. Captain Earl toiled for nearly 70 years oystering the bay, and in his retirement, he worked as the first mate and field educator on the Chesapeake Bay Foundation's floating classroom, the skipjack *Stanley Norman*. He schooled me on what he called "the black side of the bay" and "the other Chesapeake."

I distinctly remember one day with Mr. White, sitting below deck of the *Stanley Norman* docked in Annapolis harbor. He was strumming an old guitar while he talked in his wispy voice, recounting tales of what he has seen and done on the bay. He also shared with me the stories that his father and grandfather had passed along to him. As he spoke, tears ran down his cheeks.

He told me he was so glad that someone had finally stopped by that looked like him — not the typical clientele of the Chesapeake Bay Foundation. He stated that often when people wanted to interview him, they would just stick a microphone in his face and start taking pictures. They only wanted to know what it was like being a crew member on a skipjack dredging for oysters, never asking about his backstory.

But I was there with pen, paper, and a genuine interest in his life. He had to play nice to those other visitors, but he got real with me. "If you're going to tell the story of the blacks of Chesapeake," he said, "tell it straight or don't tell it at all. Tell the story of black life on the bay through ebony eyes."

In so many cases, I found that African-American stories were embedded in white American history. The white versions of successful enterprise and thriving communities that contributed to the building of America have largely overwritten the history of African Americans. Even

Black History Sharpens American History

in our contemporary era, people of color are poorly portrayed in media, have largely been absent from environmental policy development and implementation discussions, and are excluded from state resource allocations. I also see a great need for leadership at influential organizations to shift from majority-white and become more representative of our diverse American population.

Even in acknowledging all this disparity, I see a powerful reason for hope. Our society has clearly increased its focus on diversity, equity, and inclusion. These are no longer buzzwords; they are being understood as calls to action. Now is the time to grab the attention of lawmakers and inspire the leaders of tomorrow. BOCF has outlined environmental, economic, and social justice imperatives: and works to foster cross-generational interest in conservation via environmental curricula that engage urban schools with high percentages of students of color.

When we ponder the metaphorical proverb "iron sharpens iron," we see an implication of two powerful forces striking together. That is surely going to create friction, but also invariably will spark empowerment. People of all cultural, historical, and spiritual identities must be intentional in forging true mutual respect and admiration.

My fervent prayer has been that we all press on and sharpen one another, to reflect a clearer image of truth. Neither African Americans nor white Americans will ever be perfect in our journeys, but we strive to be on same one of equity, equality, and inclusion.

Charlemagne McCarter

Bestselling Author | Community Leader

Place Respect on My Name

I currently live in Greenville, NC. I am the father & grandfather of six. Some of my career highlights include being a U.S. Army Veteran, successful entrepreneur, co-author, & radio host of BRICKS CITY on WDRBmedia, iHeart, TuneIn, & Streema radio which can be downloaded to your media device.

Place Respect on My Name

Living in America today has showed us more often than not that our country is much divided. Justice and liberty seem to not apply to all. The only thing that we have is our name. Our name is the only thing that we are born with, die with, and cannot be divided. Practice this exercise-Say your name aloud! Say your name aloud again! Now think about what your name means to you. Now think about how others view your name. This small exercise carries a lot of weight. While doing an exercise like this, it makes you think about how others view you rather than how you view yourself. This is what I had to do. Growing up, family and friends called me "Keith" a shortened version of my middle name because they couldn't pronounce my first name "Charlemagne". I had to learn how to value my name, "Charlemagne". In studying the background to my name, it was derived from a respectable man who was called Charles the Great. He was known as a Warrior, later became a King, and a devout family man. Through life, I had to embrace that I have a unique name and possess the qualities of this man, though I am my own man and unique in my own way. So yes, I put respect on my own name because of who I am and who I choose to be a

Place Respect on My Name

man, father, and friend. In this passage, we are going to take a journey through hardship, self-doubt, and triumph. This journey, only your name could with-stand but that's only if you value your name as you should.

Hardship. Life tosses many obstacles. This has purpose, believe it or not. It tossed me an obstacle once they discharged me from the U.S. Army. My plans were to retire from the Army and ride off into the sunset like most happy endings. Unfortunately, my career was cut short. Once back in the civilian word I began college. It was great for a bit but was not enough for me. I fell on a mental hardship where I was trying to figure out who Charlemagne was all over again. I had a goal that I felt I could have achieved, but it was taken away—I was lost mentally. As time went by, I attempted to come up with business ideas and did not pursue them for one reason- Mentally; I was still stuck in the military. Fortunately, around this time a friend of mind offered me a job working with individuals that had mental and physical impairments. While working with these individuals, I looked at myself in a light that I had never looked at myself before-I had been ungrateful. They did not give these individuals an even playing field-physically nor mentally by no choice of their own. Yet, even in that, they still knew their name, even if

Place Respect on My Name

they could not spell it or verbalize it. At this moment, I realized I had created my own mental hardship and had a choice about my life and the outcome. It was time for me to place respect on my own name. From there, I knew that nothing would stop me from pursuing what was and is mine.

Self-Doubt. Pushing forward, I networked and develop business ideas. I traveled and meeting with executives from different organizations that I was interested in doing business. Meetings with the executives showed promise but still no contracts. Self-doubt settled in because I had done everything the right way. I attended business development classes and network sessions. This was definitely not cheap, so more money was going out than money coming in, which was creating more room for disaster. During a vulnerable time, a few companies approached me about partnering because of some socioeconomic status that I had. After researching these companies, I found out that I could have possibly made millions, but I felt as if I would have lost some respect on my name by allowing myself to deal with companies not built on integrity. Situations made me really have to soul search for what was important to me- millions in my pocket or no have face value when I look in the mirror. I chose face value without even a second thought. I understood and now

Place Respect on My Name

understand even more the repercussions of selling myself. My integrity is more important to me than money, and I would never knowingly do anything to damage it. Self-doubt slowly was pushed to the side for self-love and keeping respect on my name.

Triumph. By now, a few years have passed, and I began working 12-hour rotating shifts at night. With my dreams still intact, I continued emailing, making phone calls, and attending events when I could. Once again, I started back working with individuals with mental and physical impairments. Years passing felt like centuries as my hope was almost lost until one day, I received an email saying, "Your bid was accepted." Triumph... finally! Now, all the hard work had paid off. My first contract with the government was three hundred thousand dollars ($300,000). As with any business or job, you have gross pay and net pay. My net was way lower than three hundred thousand dollars ($300,000) but I was grateful knowing that I could overcome the obstacles I faced while keeping my name respectfully intact. After I received that first contract, I received more contracts from different agencies. In one of my better years, I accumulated three million dollars ($3,000,000) in contracts in one year. The Department of Agriculture recognized me to speak as a panelist at a conference at North Carolina Central

Place Respect on My Name

University. I spoke with small business owners as well as students about how to do business with the Department of Agriculture. Definitely, I was humbled to receive such recognition for my hard work and determination while keeping respect on my name. While living a respectful life and running a business built on integrity, it has given me the opportunity to become a co-author of a bestselling anthology entitled, "When Men Lean In". Over 1000 copies have been printed, and I personally sold over 100 copies. This book tells the real-life story of how 13 other men endured the struggles of life and have become triumphant black men. I am also a radio personality, "The Real Charlemagne". My radio show developed with the purpose to give and bring the community together, to bring awareness, to give local leaders a platform, and to showcase small businesses. Yes, "The Real Charlemagne" is who I am. I place respect on my name so much so that I am branding it, which allows others to place respect on my name and to see me for the real man that I am!

The emotional rollercoaster of life left me with many bumps and bruises and sleepless nights, but I remained encouraged. I had to learn how to trust the process, not the "now" situation. "Charlemagne" is my name by birth and the

Place Respect on My Name

name that will be on my tombstone. Your name will have the same transition as mine from birth to the grave. In closing, remember to place respect on your name so others will amplify your name in praise while you are here in the natural as well as when you have transitioned to the other side. So, make your life proud & your name worth saying loud!

Contact me at Charlemagnenow@gmail.com for more information or to be a guest on my radio talk show which is on WDRBmedia, iHeart, TuneIn, Streema and airs every Saturday at 12 noon.

Natalie Degraffinreaidt

Award Winning-Entrepreneur | Wellness Expert

Living in The Moment

Living in The Moment

Living in the moment takes a lot of patience and trust in God. We always remember that patience is a virtue. Our process is building our stamina and character to endure.

The process is necessary for our own growth. I understand the uncertainty of waiting. Every level serves a purpose in our lives. It's our job to gain the knowledge necessary on each level in order to graduate to the next. If you don't pass the test on the first level, you definitely won't be equipped for the next level.

For an example, a child must attend Preschool, Kindergarten, 1st grade, 2nd grade, etc. However, the child must pass each grade before getting promoted to the next grade!

If the teacher sees the child not properly grasping or learning the lesson being taught on that particular level… unfortunately, the child won't get promoted.

I truly hope everyone understands the point in that terminology. Each level has a lesson specifically for that child to learn and master before getting promoted to the next level.

Hypothetically speaking, each grade serves a major part in the process to better equip the child for his/her next phase on the journey.

We can't skip 1st grade and go straight to 12th grade. I am not sure about anyone else, but I can speak to myself. In my youth days, I always wanted to rush my process. In elementary school, I remembered wanting to be in middle school. The middle school children seem to have a better advantage in more freedom! I

Living in The Moment

didn't think about the process those older children had to endure before being promoted to that level.

Their level attracted me not the process of reaching that level.

Let me talk a little about the now! I truly understand everyone is on different levels in life. One thing I beg of you is to never discredit someone else's process.

We should never be shallow on this journey. We must always seek understanding by gaining the proper knowledge in order to grow and learn.

I would like to take a moment to testify about myself. My life is an open book. I am an instrument used by God, so being transparent is imperative for me on this journey.

I am constantly learning how to live in the moment and not rush my process. Many times, I tried to achieve things before the proper timing. We must remember there is a reason and season for everything in life. It's imperative to know the seasons of life.

It'll help you get a better understanding of your process and gain more patience along the way. I didn't always understand this, nor didn't care to understand.

Natalie knew what she wanted on her journey and moved in haste. This mindset didn't always work for me and caused many detours in my life.

Living in The Moment

Being a visionary is never easy. I could clearly see the vision God given me, but didn't want to endure the process.

Believe me when I tell you!! God is a good, good father and ultimate teacher! A father protects their children and chastises them when necessary.

He will never set us up to fail! I knew God has called me to the healing ministry, along with being a successful business owner. However, I tried rushing into being a business owner, rushing into ministry without properly going through the steps.

God detoured me to complete unfinished lessons before getting promoted to the next level. Everything was in black and white for me. My focus was wrong.

I missed plenty valuable lessons and repeated certain tests multiple times due to me not living in the moment. We must learn to appreciate the process! It's actually creating a better version of you!

I've learned now to never cease the moment! Always continue to be a student of life. Take advantage of every opportunity on your journey. Stay humble and trust God!

Proverbs 3:5-5 Trust God with all thine heart and lean not on your own understanding in all your ways acknowledge him and he shall direct your paths! The key word is "Trust"!

We must trust God with our whole heart! God will never leave us nor forsake us! He wants us to prosper in every area of our lives.

Living in The Moment

I know for myself the more "Natalie" surrendered her plans to God, the more he could move on my behalf! There is no way we can get what God has for us without following his lead!

We must continue to get out of our own way! We as humans become our biggest hindrance! There's no need to rush your process!

What God has for you is for you! God has worked miracles on my behalf, but it took me getting out of my own way! He has made all crooked places straight for me!

I know for a fact that God will do the same for you! Don't be consumed with the vision and arriving at your destiny without enjoying the process.

Remember to enjoy yourself, love on yourself, appreciate the process, grow on every level! Most importantly, live in the moment!

Each level is serving you a purpose and preparing you for the next level. God is increasing your borders, so he needs to stretch you beyond capacity!

I am forever grateful for the healing God brought into my life. I am forever grateful for my lessons in life. I am forever grateful for God choosing me!

I am forever grateful for God's perfect timing for our lives. When it's your harvest season, God will have people lined up to help propel you to greatness!

Living in The Moment

Trust me, God knows the blueprint for your life! Just follow him!

In my closing of this chapter, just remember this…God haven't forgotten about you! In -fact, God is waiting on you! He wants to bless your life! Seek God for yourself! In Christ is where your true being is!

Remember, never to compete with others! You should only compete to being a better version of yourself! Remember to never cease the moment. Never rush your process and live in the now. Remember to be open to change and accept change for your life. Stay humble and most importantly, trust God on your journey! Remember to not judge people and to see people through the lens of Christ. Remember not to think too highly of yourself and miss the mark!

Pride comes before the fall! God resists the proud, but gives grace to the humble! Remember to love you, accept yourself, and forgive yourself daily! You are more than enough! Remember to always combat the enemy within with greatness!

God has affirmed you, so you are free to fly!

I thank you for taking the time out to read this chapter! Living in the moment brought so much peace and clarity to my life! I know it will do the same for each and every reader! Blessings to all of you! Remember, you will arrive at your destiny, but live in the moment! It's leading to your destiny!

Natalie Degraffinreaidt

blossomingseedsproduction.com

Jackie "Hollywood" Mims

Entrepreneur | Public Speaker | Coach, Media Host |

Visionary Author

Faith, Hope & Love Part II

"Exercise Your Faith Daily"

Faith, Hope & Love Part II

"Exercise Your Faith Daily"

"Iron sharpens Iron; so, a man sharpeneth the countenance of his friend"-Proverbs 27:17"

I am truly blessed and extremely grateful to be a part of volume I Iron Sharpens Iron. I want to start by personally thanking Dr. Larry White Sr for this tremendous opportunity to share my heart. It was a privilege to write the last chapter of the volume I, "Faith Hope & Love." I am anchoring volume II with an unexpected continuation of my story. During that time of writing the last chapter my mother Frances Mims was fighting for her life with COVID-19 on a ventilator at Peconic Bay Hospital on Long Island, NY. My mother's fight with COVID ended eight days after her arrival at Peconic Bay Hospital. I want to share with you how eight days can change your life forever and leave you with a gaping hole in your heart.

Losing our dear mother, the matriarch of my family, and the centerpiece of our hearts was devastating. The pain is still raw for us. She was a beautiful woman of God, full of life, love and laughter. She exercised her faith daily, and she was so thankful to God for blessing her down through the years. Mom believed that prayer is a muscle that you must flex and use every single day. Like you exercise your mind and body, you must also exercise your faith.

My sister Vanessa and Mom lived together, and Vanessa came in from work feeling terrible. COVID was new and on the rise.

Faith, Hope & Love Part II

"Exercise Your Faith Daily"

Right away Mom agreed to move to our brother Ralph's home, which was a few minutes away, until Vanessa felt better. Vanessa did adversely test positive for Covid and she battled for 20 plus days at home suffering in her bed. Of course, mom and all of us called to check on her. She really couldn't talk too much because she was struggling with her breathing, fevers, loss of memory, body aches, and pains associated with COVID-19. Mom was so concerned about her and continued to pray without ceasing. During my sister's recovery, they took Mom to the oncologist for her regular appointment to receive her iron infusions because she was anemic. Upon arriving at her doctor's office, Mom walked into her appointment.

After completing her vital signs, doctors noticed her oxygen level was very low and suggested that she go to the emergency room by ambulance. That was the last time my family saw our dear mother. When my mom arrived, they thought it was COVID related, but it was not confirmed. They immediately admitted her to the hospital and shared in the morning with me she was on 100% oxygen and struggled to breathe through the night. I spoke with the doctor and she suggested the ventilator right away and hydroxychloroquine, along with lots of other medications. My sister and I along with a close family friend Rick Black, a registered nurse of 30 years, assisted with calling the hospital day and night to get progress reports for our family. Day two we could have a family video chat so we could see mom's beautiful face on the ventilator. We called her name and her eyes opened. She looked around, hearing our loving familiar voices saying

Faith, Hope & Love Part II

"Exercise Your Faith Daily"

how much we loved her and hurry home we miss you. My heart is still paining, and eyes fill with tears at the memory of seeing our mother's eyes open. It gave us so much hope and inspiration. It was heartbreaking to see our mother in that condition. I am still broken to this day.

On day number three and four, we could Facetime and see our mother again. Her eyes were weak, and she was struggling. On the fourth day, we had a prayer call with Pastor Natalie R. Wimberly of Clinton Memorial AME Zion Church, Greenport, N.Y. We also invited other pastors, friends, family members and the community to pray for our mom affectionately known as "Nana," one of the mothers of the church.

During this time, Mom showed some signs of improvement, but she was still on the ventilator. We continued to call day and night. Sunday, April 5, 2020, the doctor shared that she was not improving but declining just that fast. On Monday I received a call from the doctor, and she shared with me to get in touch with our family because it was time to say goodbye to your mother. I quickly called my sister Vanessa and Rick, and we spoke back to the doctor. She confirmed they did all they could for Mom.

I cannot describe the pain we felt saying goodbye to the most beautiful person with the biggest heart in the world. I felt like my heart shattered in a million pieces. I called the family, and we gathered on Facetime for the last time to say goodbye to the love of our life. We all told her how much we love her, and we will

Faith, Hope & Love Part II

"Exercise Your Faith Daily"

miss her so much. Life will never be the same without her. I heard everyone saying what was in their hearts. At 7:00 p.m. the doctor called and said, "Your mother passed with dignity and peace. May God rest her soul."

After our hearts were ripped out of our chest, we were told because of COVID-19 we could not see her body. During that time, the body was wrapped, and they gave us two choices. The crematorium or burial. Our mother's wish was granted, crematorium. In a matter of eight days, she was gone. No physical contact. No time to prepare ourselves. Currently, my family and I are living with a gaping hole in our hearts, an emptiness, because there is no closure, but we have faith.

Losing a loved one to COVID-19 is extremely painful. Sitting at the dining room table looking at an empty chair that your loved one once occupied is very difficult. That is the most difficult and challenging part. When I go home to Greenport, N.Y and pull into the driveway, I miss seeing her beautiful smile, and her arms open wide, ready to embrace us. I had to gather myself by walking into the house again for the first time without her being there. I walked by her room and it smelled like Angel, her favorite perfume. Her hats for church and all her Bible scriptures are still in her room. Visions of seeing her at her knee bench brings back memories of hymns, scripture and prayers that she raised us on. It's like she is still here. I miss her so much. My family and I are hurting, and we realize that a half-million plus is still hurting and broken. My prayers are with all the family. I

Faith, Hope & Love Part II

"Exercise Your Faith Daily"

know that my family and I are surviving every day through the love of Jesus Christ. She would sharpen our iron daily, teaching us the importance of prayer and to call on the Lord. Trust God's love daily. She exercised her faith every single day. She looked forward to dwelling in the house of the Lord every Sunday. I am proud to say that Mom lived and studied the word of God, and she lived every day for Christ and her family. She lived and believed in the word *"PUSH - Pray Until Something Happens."*

Please keep my family along with countless other families who lost loved ones to COVID-19 in your prayers. Remember to exercise your faith daily. God will reward you for your faithfulness and comfort you in times of need. I want to speak to someone's heart right now and encourage you with one of my mom's favorite scripture she recited daily. Psalm 91.

"He that dwelleth in the secret place of the most high God shall abide under the shadows of the almighty. I will say of the Lord he is my refuge and my fortress My God in him I will trust. Surely, he shall deliver thee from the snare of the fowler, and from the noisome pestilence. He shall cover thee with his feathers, and under his wings shalt thou trust, his truth shall be thy shield and buckler. Thou shalt not be afraid for the terror by night nor for the arrows that flieth by day nor for the pestilence that walketh in darkness nor for the destruction that wasteth at noonday. A thousand may fall at thy side, and ten thousand shall fall at thy right hand but it shall not come nigh thee. Only with thine eyes shalt thou behold and see the reward of the wicked.

Faith, Hope & Love Part II

"Exercise Your Faith Daily"

Because thou hast made the Lord, who is my refuge, even the most high your dwelling place, nor evil shall befall you, nor shall any plague come near your dwelling; for he shall give his angels charge over you, to keep you in all your ways. In their hands they shall bear you up, lest you dash your foot against a stone, you shall tread upon the lion and cobra, the young lion and the serpent you shall trample underfoot. Because he has set his love upon me, therefore I will deliver him; I will set him on high because he has known my name. He shall call upon me, and I will answer him; I will be with him in trouble; I will deliver him and honor him. With long life, I will satisfy him, and show him my salvation."

Let your light shine as you leave your footprint everywhere you go! Thank you!

Jackie "Hollywood" Mims

jackiemims.com

***Conclusion ***

We hope that this book, Iron Sharpens Iron: ***Inspired To Achieve, Think, & Grow,*** has helped you and continues to support you on your journey to greatness. In reading each chapter, you should have captured and journaled information that will allow you to move forward with your vision. The stories, sharing, and experience should have left you with an action plan to execute what you desire to become personally, professionally, as a leader, or in your business.

The direction and creative intelligence of these authors should have provided insight to achieving your goals, choose wise counsel, and overcome difficult circumstances. Now that you have put your head together with masterminds featured in this book, your ideas, creativeness, and dreams are ready to come to fruition. Your iron should be sharpened, and your mindset in awareness of greatness.

Social justice, equity, and tolerance are not just words; they are benchmarks for excellence during this time of a Pandemic. We must work together continuously to provide resources and access to information for the youth in urban areas leading up to higher education. During this pandemic, peaceful demonstrations, and the innocent killings and shootings of our young black men and women, we must be remember the ultimate sacrifice has come with a cost, and the way out of the mayhem is to vote in efforts to raise the awareness for social injustice across our Nation.

As National chair of Signature Entrepreneurs & Mastermind Group for the past 5 years, I have learned a great deal of responsibility for serving others and cultivating a team. Upon assembling the Masterminds in 2016, I felt a great need to support leaders and entrepreneurs with an intent of creating leaders and creating vision. Being a Visionary Author for this project brings my mission and vision into perspective in efforts to learn from others and collaborate with great minds. This collaboration with our mastermind members has already moved some of our members out of their comfort zone and giving them the insight of walking into their purpose.

The ability to work together as a functioning group takes perseverance, patience, and faith. Faith allows us to stay committed while on the journey until the blessings come down. The Lord will often say "yes" to our prayers, he will often say "no" and will often say "wait!"

Dr. Larry White Sr.

International | National Chairman

Contributing Authors

Dr. Larry White Sr.

Jackie "Hollywood" Mims

Lisa Jones Harwell

R. Wesley Webb

Leah Chapman

Eric A. Lomax

Dr. Paul W. Dyer

Gina Goree-Hitchens

Demetrica "Meechie" Jefferis

Natalie Degraffinreaidt

Charlemagne McCarter

Cortne' Lee Smith

Eve Gomez

Vincent O. Leggett

Tiffany Williams-Parra

Dr. Clarice Kavanaugh

Toya Jordan

Senita V. Carter

www.ingramcontent.com/pod-product-compliance
Lightning Source LLC
Chambersburg PA
CBHW012107090526
44592CB00019B/2683